MESOLITHIC PRELUDE

$\vee$

MESOLITHIC PRELUDE

THE PALAEOLITHIC–NEOLITHIC TRANSITION IN OLD WORLD PREHISTORY

GRAHAME CLARK

at the University Press
EDINBURGH

© J.G.D.Clark 1980
EDINBURGH UNIVERSITY PRESS
22 George Square, Edinburgh

ISBN 0 85224 365 0

Set in Monotype Ehrhardt by
Speedspools, Edinburgh
and printed in Great Britain by
The Scolar Press, Ilkley

> *Contents* <

Preface p.vii

> *Preface* <

The challenge of an invitation to address an audience as well-informed as that which customarily attends lectures on the Robert Munro Foundation at Edinburgh frequently stimulates trains of thought that extend beyond what can readily be contained in the lecture form. This applies all the more when, as in the present case, only one lecture was involved. On the other hand ideas, as distinct from information or instruction, may often be conveyed more effectively in small books or extended essays than in a weightier volume.

The theme to which I have addressed myself, the continuity of history and of the Stone Age in particular, is one that for historical reasons is particularly relevant to Europe and contiguous parts of south-west Asia. Yet it is of no less importance as a guide to research over those extensive parts of the world that escaped the worst distortions of stadial archaeology. Modern research into the process of domestication and the results that have already accrued from the world-wide application of radiocarbon dating are only two of the factors to underline the crucial importance of the Mesolithic, Archaic or Intermediate phase of the Stone Age in the history of mankind. It was during this phase, however designated, that steps were taken crucial to the emergence in different parts of the world of the several distinctive and diverse civilisations of man. The results already obtained in parts of south-west Asia, Mesoamerica and Peru should encourage those currently researching on the emergence of major foci of civilisation in south Asia and the Far East in particular. For Europeans investigation of the Mesolithic is vital above all for a correct understanding of the later prehistory of their own continent.

I am grateful to the editorial staff of the Edinburgh University Press for the way they have reconciled the need to combine the documentation sought by specialists with a text reasonably accessible to readers with more general interests. Not least I must thank my wife once again for her detailed help in editing the text.

Grahame Clark
Peterhouse

INTRODUCTION

The prime object of this book is to examine critically the century-old division of the Stone Age into Old and New, the Palaeolithic and the Neolithic, and to suggest that this dichotomy is not merely overdrawn, but an impediment to a just understanding of what happened in prehistory. It is the broad ecological approach foreshadowed in the Munro lectures of thirty years ago and developed in *Prehistoric Europe : the economic basis*[1] that allows us to see the need to explore with greater effect the essential continuity of prehistory.

It is hardly necessary to recall that the terms Palaeolithic and Neolithic were originally defined by Sir John Lubbock, later Lord Avebury, in his *Prehistoric Times* (1865). On the other hand, in view of the convention that terms ought to be deployed in their original sense so long as they remain in use, it is perhaps worth reminding ourselves that Lubbock employed three criteria for distinguishing the Neolithic from the Palaeolithic. Each of these needs to be satisfied for a valid definition. Palaeontologically, and therefore chronologically, Neolithic man was a contemporary of extant or recently extant animals and plants, whereas his predecessors of the Palaeolithic at least overlapped with extinct species. Economically, Palaeolithic

1. As stated at the end of the preface to *Prehistoric Europe : The Economic Basis* (Clark 1952a) that work took shape from the Munro Lectures that I gave in Edinburgh in February 1949. For a recent review of the ecological approach in both its synchronic and diachronic aspects, see my inaugural Gordon Childe Memorial Lecture 'Prehistory since Childe' (Clark 1976).

man was thought of as subsisting exclusively by hunting, fishing and foraging, whereas Neolithic man lived at least in part by cultivating crops and domesticating livestock. Lastly, there were differences in technology. Two of the most prominent of these included the practice of polishing the blades of flint and stone axes by Neolithic man and his adoption of pottery as a means of supplementing and to some extent replacing containers made of other materials. Lubbock was particularly impressed by the contrast between what was recovered from Palaeolithic cave deposits like those explored by Lartet and Christy (1875) in Perigord as recently as 1860–63,[2] and what had come to light some years before when the levels in the Swiss lakes fell so dramatically in the winter of 1853–54 to reveal what French prehistorians soon came to term the Robenhausian.[3] The contrast to which Lubbock drew such pointed attention led the French prehistorians A. and G. de Mortillet (1881) to emphasise at least a hiatus in our knowledge of European prehistory. Gabriel even went so far in a chapter on the hiatus written only a few years later (de Mortillet 1883, 478–84) as to marshal fifteen differences under climatic, demographic and psychic as well as palaeontological, economic and technological heads, the effect of which was to create a veritable chasm, at least in Europe, between the Palaeolithic and the Neolithic. It will be our contention in this work to show that subsequent research has bridged what was long perceived as a gap or disconformity in prehistory.

As Hugo Obermaier (1924, 322) dryly remarked of the hiatus hypothesis applied to Europe, 'it would indeed be strange if man should have deserted that continent at the very time when its climatic conditions were becoming increasingly favourable'. In fact, within five years of the definition of the hiatus E. Piette (1889, 203) began to demonstrate the con-

2. E. Lartet and H. Christy carried out their excavations between 1860 and 1863, but their results were not published, in the event posthumously, until 1875.
3. The results, communicated by F. Keller to the Anthropological Society of Zürich between 1854 and 1863, were made available in English in Keller (1866).

tinuity of European settlement by excavating a distinctive assemblage of archaeological material stratified between Late Magdalenian and Neolithic levels in the cave of Mas d'Azil, Ariège, material that could hardly be classified as either Palaeolithic or Neolithic. When more up-to-date textbooks on prehistoric archaeology began to be written after the 1914–18 war, it became necessary to allocate space to assemblages which, to quote Obermaier again, 'properly speaking, are post-Palaeolithic and pre-Neolithic'. This in turn required a short-hand term for ease of reference. In those parts of the Old World where Lubbock's basic terminology was in common use the logical one was 'Mesolithic', a term applied abortively as long ago as 1872 (Westropp 1872, 102–4) to bridge the gap between the earlier and later phases of the Palaeolithic, and in its modern sense already by Allen Brown (1893) to denote a flint assemblage that he supposed to be intermediate in age between the Old and the New Stone Ages. Brown entitled his paper prophetically 'On the continuity of the Neolithic and Palaeolithic periods'.

My former teacher Miles Burkitt (1925, 5; 1926, ch.1) was one of the first prehistorians to apply the term Mesolithic systematically to assemblages intermediate in age between the Palaeolithic and Neolithic, as defined by Lubbock. When I myself began to research in 1930 British archaeology remained to a large extent in the first phase of its classificatory era and was still preoccupied with establishing bare chronological sequences. My own concern was to fill the gap 'between the close of the Pleistocene and the arrival of the Neolithic arts in this country' (Clark 1932, 5), a task sufficiently daunting when the definition of the Neolithic in Britain was still hazy to say the least, when radiocarbon dating lay a full generation ahead and even pollen analysis was only just beginning to penetrate from Sweden. Interestingly enough, when Childe (1947) finally brought himself to make even a sparing use of the term Mesolithic to denote intermediate assemblages he did so 'because in time – but only in time – they occupy a place between the latest palaeolithic and the oldest neolithic culture'.

3

To understand why Childe was so qualified in his use of such a convenient term, and why other respected authorities could never bring themselves even to qualified acceptance, it is important to remember that Lubbock was himself a Victorian evolutionist: as I was at pains to point out above, his terminology carried from the outset economic and technological as well as chronological connotations. Childe was thus not the first or only prehistorian to invest his terminology with cultural historical overtones. Hugo Obermaier was quite specific in rejecting the term Mesolithic on the ground that it could be justified only if it could be shown to display 'a natural evolutionary development – a progressive transformation from Palaeolithic to Neolithic'. As Childe was to do soon after, he preferred to term most transitional assemblages Epi-palaeolithic on the score that they were 'posthumous descendants of the Palaeolithic', reserving the term Protoneolithic for later manifestations presaging the Neolithic. In Childe's case it is likely that he shared another, specifically Marxist outgrowth from evolutionist notions. Certainly he believed that period terms gained in significance if linked with 'vital stages in human progress' and served to draw 'attention to real revolutions that affected all departments of human life' (Childe 1935a). Childe was fully cognisant of and in fact drew inspiration from Lewis H. Morgan's scheme for the stadial development of human society set out in his *Ancient Society* (1877). This in turn had strongly influenced Engels' *The Origin of the Family, Private Property and the State* (1884), itself the inspiration for the scheme of prehistory once enforced in the Soviet Union. During N. Y. Marr's directorship of the Institute of the History of Material Culture at Moscow (1930–34) a scheme was laid down whereby human history was held to comprise five stages in social evolution defined one from another by a series of quantum jumps (see Mongait 1959, 57). Childe's Neolithic Revolution was one such jump. He viewed the change from Palaeolithic to Neolithic as revolutionary in the same way as Soviet prehistorians at that time regarded the jump from Primitive Community to Matriarchal Class Society.

No wonder that Childe should have found it hard to treat the transitional assemblages as anything more than the fag-end of the preceding era and why, even when ready to admit the Mesolithic as defining a space of time, he felt compelled to deny its status as marking a substantive phase in prehistory.

If in the west the Mesolithic was nevertheless accepted, though with varying degrees of enthusiasm, as at lowest a convenient label for designating assemblages that could hardly be accommodated in the classification inherited from Lubbock, in the Soviet Union it was for long systematically ignored as something irrelevant because incapable of throwing useful light on the course of social change. By one of those ironies of which history is composed, the present new-found interest in the Mesolithic of the Old World stems precisely from the fact that it is now perceived to be of crucial significance for understanding the course of prehistory, and not least for explaining the rise and spread of the Neolithic societies that laid the foundations of the diverse civilisations of mankind.

In a society such as the Soviet Union in which archaeological, like all other intellectual activities are geared directly to the prevailing political ideology, it is hardly surprising that the turn-about, when it came, was far more abrupt than in the West or that its immediate occasion was itself political. Whereas the Mesolithic was ignored so long as Marrist ideas were still dominant, the overthrow of these ideas after the 1939–45 war resulted in its rapid promotion to a key place in research. The principal factor here, of course, was the stimulation of patriotic feeling as a weapon against the Nazi invaders, even if the change was justified in doctrinal terms. When Stalin personally attacked Marrist doctrines in his *Marxism and the Problems of Philology* (1950) he did so ostensibly on the ground that they ran counter to true Marxism. Marr's name was removed from the Institute and his work pilloried as 'vulgar sociology'. National and racial variations, previously suppressed for detracting from the scientific view of history as the unfolding of an inevitable social process, were now appreciated as contributing to national identity and awareness. But the essence of national history was that it must be shown to be continuous. There was no room for gaps or even for quantum jumps. As Mongait expressed the matter in his widely-read book of 1959, 'Marr's followers (had) fitted the data of material sources by ready-made, prepared schemes. Works were published in which it was asserted that as a result of a leap, by means of a miraculous transformation, one people changed into another . . .'.[4] It is significant that Mongait (1961, 85f) should already have envisaged that 'the transition to a new historical epoch . . . gradually took place in the post-glacial age'. He explained the brevity of his treatment of this now important phase in prehistory by noting that 'much less is known in the world about the Mesolithic than about the other periods of the Stone Age'. The significant point is that Mongait should have used the previously eschewed word 'Mesolithic' in a work designed for a wide public. Professional archaeologists in the Soviet Union soon began to concern themselves with a phase of prehistory that they were increasingly coming to view as one of major historical importance. M. V. Voevodskii (1950) summarised the Mesolithic of eastern Europe; A. A. Formazov (1955) discussed the periodisation of Mesolithic sites in European Russia; and only a few years after Mongait's book the movement was powerfully advanced by a volume of papers under the editorship of I. I. Gurina (1966) ranging over much of Russia and extending, in an important paper by V. M. Masson, over south-west Asia. Finally, the wheel of Soviet archaeology turned full circle when G. I. Mathyushin (1976) began his book on the Mesolithic of the South Urals by apostrophising the period as 'the most important epoch in history'. This was a far cry indeed from ignoring this phase completely or treating it as a mere epilogue of the Palaeolithic as was customary before 1950. Mathyushin accorded the Mesolithic such a high degree of historical importance because he viewed it as bridging the transition from economies based exclusively

4. M. W. Thompson, Translator's Foreword to the 1961 Pelican edition of Mongait (1959), 3of. For a review of Russian attitudes to the Mesolithic, see Clark (1978).

on hunting, fishing, fowling and foraging to one that depended to a greater or lesser extent on farming, the ultimate basis of civilisation.

Although on a number of matters Mathyushin's book, which reached me while preparing this work, calls for critical review, his general position is close to that which I have myself taught for many years and (admittedly only summarily) maintained in print since 1952 (Clark 1952b, 325; 1953; 1967, esp. 111ff; 1970, 85ff; 1978). The time is now ripe to expound and justify the proposition that the Mesolithic, so far from being a dead end, was in fact an essential prelude to fundamental advances in the development of culture. The reasons why this was only recently admitted in the U.S.S.R. have just been discussed. In the west the explanation for its tardy recognition lies to a large extent in the history of the subject. Serious work on the definition of the Mesolithic, as of the Palaeolithic and Neolithic, was first undertaken in Europe, that is in a territory that has proved to have been marginal to the focal area of economic change between *c.* 10000 and 5000 B.C. It is no wonder that the profile of the Mesolithic drawn in the chapters conscientiously devoted to it in the various books Childe (1925, ch.1; 1935b, ch.2) wrote before the 1939–45 war on British and European prehistory was a low one. The impression his readers were likely to form was that of survivors from the Ice Age living on at a miserably low level of culture against the time of enlightenment issuing from revolutionary change in south-west Asia. In the circumstances that prevailed when Childe was writing many of his books this attitude was understandable enough. The evidence summarised by Miles Burkitt in 1925 was convincing but hardly exciting, and my own study (Clark 1932) of the situation in Britain carried out under his supervision amounted to little more than a typological study of flint assemblages supplemented by occasional artefacts of antler and bone. No one appreciated this more painfully than the author, which is why he turned to northern Europe. (For the limitations under which *The Mesolithic Age in Britain* was written, see Clark 1972a, 3f.)

2

MESOLITHIC
TRANSFORMATION IN
SOUTH-WEST ASIA

Definition of 'The Gap'

The extension of modern prehistoric research to south-west Asia was delayed until the break-down of the Ottoman Empire as an outcome of the First World War. Two main groups of prehistorians entered the field. Although both concerned primarily with establishing the chronological sequence of early settlement over the territory between the Mediterranean Sea and the Iranian plateau, their operations, while overlapping, were largely independent. On the one hand were those, pioneered by Dorothy Garrod, concerned first and foremost with establishing the Stone Age sequence from the Middle Palaeolithic through the Upper Palaeolithic to the terminal hunter-forager stage represented in Palestine by the Natufian (Garrod and Bate 1937, 1942; Garrod 1957) and in Kurdistan by the Zarzian (Garrod 1930). On the other hand, there were those, including on the British side Leonard Woolley, Kathleen Kenyon, Max Mallowan and Seton Lloyd, interested first and foremost with tracing the origins of settled civilisations by exploring the successive levels of tells from the cities and structures of literate polities down to the earliest villages.

It was precisely the contrast between the state of affairs exemplified in the Natufian and Zarzian phases of Near Eastern prehistory and that reflected in the tells, that stimulated Gordon Childe to formulate and proclaim the hypothesis of the Neolithic Revolution. Conversely when, with the 1939–

45 war over and Henri Frankfort's seminar behind it, the Oriental Institute of the University of Chicago assumed the lead and reanimated research into the origins of civilisation in south-west Asia, a prime stimulus was admitted to have been Childe's hypothesis (Braidwood 1973). Already in 1945 the 'gap chart' drawn up at the Institute for undergraduate instruction served to dramatise the dearth of information about what had gone forward during the interval between the terminal hunter-fisher phase and the beginning of settled life, giving rise to the formation of tells in south-west Asia. In European terms, which admittedly Robert Braidwood in large measure repudiated (Braidwood and Howe 1960, 4 n.1),[1] the Chicago team set out to fill the gap between Lubbock's Palaeolithic and Neolithic or, in de Mortillet's terms, to test the existence of a hiatus.

The excavations undertaken by the Oriental Institute of Chicago and those inspired by its initiative, accomplished far more than extending the stratigraphy of a region of key importance to the history of civilisation. As befits fieldwork undertaken to test ideas, the campaign as a whole has helped to alter the whole climate of thought about the true nature of the process of economic transformation at one time telescoped in the slogan 'The Neolithic Revolution'. Indeed the Chicago initiative was one of those most influential in transforming prehistory from a hobby into a disciplined field of scholarship uniquely equipped to test historical hypotheses in terms of extended periods of time.

DOMESTICATION AS PROCESS

This makes it appropriate to preface a review of research in south-west Asia by taking note of parallel fieldwork and thinking on the key problem of how the changes in subsistence, rightly defined by Childe as crucial to the emergence of the

1. The dislike of neo-Grecisms indicated in the footnote cited is conspicuously absent from the hard sciences, but leaving that aside it is hardly logical to retain one of Lubbock's terms ('Palaeolithic'), even after 'some soul-searching', without the other ('Neolithic').

several civilisations of mankind, and not least of our own, actually unfolded. From Childe's original standpoint it is indeed ironic that attention is currently being redirected to the Mesolithic as the age in which this crucial transformation was first accomplished and then enabled to spread. By a further irony the most elegant demonstration of the transition from hunter-gatherer to farming economies has been contributed by New World archaeologists for whom 'Mesolithic' is a super-fluous term.

New World archaeologists have never had to confront a notional gap or hiatus in settlement. It has long been accepted that the Palaeoindians, like their Upper Palaeolithic counterparts in Europe, relied substantially on hunting wild animals, including some of extinct species. Again, the succeeding Archaic has been regarded as a period when men adapted to Neothermal conditions by establishing increasingly close relations, more particularly with plants, relations that culminated in full domestication. Finally, the deployment of fully developed systems of food-production has been seen as providing an early Formative phase of more developed polities disposing of elaborate architecture, specialised crafts and in some cases writing. For present purposes interest focuses on the intermediate phase, the Archaic, equivalent in a broad sense to our Mesolithic.

Systematic investigation of the development of this was begun by R.S. MacNeish and his team in the Valley of Tehuacan, Central Mexico, in 1960 (Byers 1967). It is significant that one of the chief aims was to test P.C. Mangelsdorf's hypothesis on the genesis of maize, the most important food plant of the New World. The reason why MacNeish, and in due course Kent Flannery working on a parallel project in the Oaxaca Valley, chose the central highlands of Mexico was that maize was only likely to have flourished in territories where the winters were sufficiently arid to have inhibited growth until the danger of frost was over. (For accessible sources to the literature see Bushnell 1977, Hammond 1977.) Moreover it was only there that valley margin caves were to be found with deposits dry enough to conserve actual traces of plants in adequate quantities. In the event remarkably complete samples were obtained of the animal and plant food consumed from the Late Pleistocene up to the time when agriculture was practised on the basis of artificial irrigation. The findings in the Mexican highlands acquired added significance in that they were strikingly confirmed, as Warwick Bray (1976, 88f) has so clearly brought out, by the investigation of sites in the Ayacucho Basin, Peru (figure 1).

It is evident that the early Archaic populations of Meso-america had a wide-ranging and intimate knowledge of potential food resources and were adept at scheduling their use throughout the year so as to yield the maximum return with the minimum of risk. The palaeontological record demon-strates that changes in relationships between men, animals and plants were not merely gradual but varied as between one species and another. Although certain plants showed signs of genetic change even in early levels, these were to begin with comparatively slight. Conversely some species retained their pristine form throughout. Avocado gave indications of genetic change as early as the El Riego phase in the Tehuacan sequence (figure 2). Squash was probably being cultivated before the end of this period and chili pepper, bottle gourds and beans during the course of the Coxcatlan.

The origin of maize, to judge from its varieties domesticated in several different localities, is still open to debate. If the recent suggestion that it was derived from a genetically related form, teosinte, proves to be correct, it follows that the small maize cobs from the beginning of the Coxcatlan phase, once attributed to a hypothetical wild species, should be interpreted as marking an early phase in domestication. What is in any case striking (Byers 1967, 190 and fig.122) is the progressive increase in the size of maize cob (from 22 to 55 mm long) and in the number of spikelets (55 to 163), a vivid illustration of the potential increase in basic food supply made possible by more intensive cultivation. The Mexican highlands were themselves one of the main centres of maize domestication. It is also

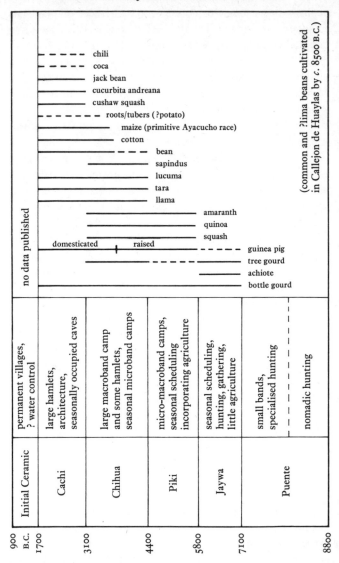

Figure 1. Evolution of settlement and subsistence in the Ayacucho Basin, Peru, 7100–1700 B.C. (after Bray).

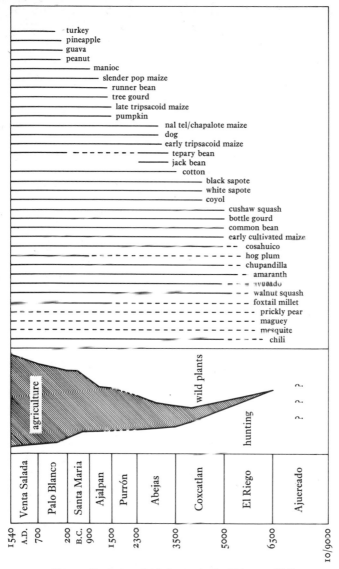

Figure 2. Evolution of subsistence in the Tehuacan Valley, central Mexico, 6500 B.C.-A.D. 1540 (after Bray).

evident that other plants that appear relatively late in the sequence reached the area in developed form. Thus cotton, domesticated long previously in Peru, did not arrive until the Ajalpan phase and manioc, a domesticate of Amazonia, until the Santa Maria phase in Tehuacan. The fact that even in Mesoamerica and South America there were several distinct foci of plant domestication confirms that this was an outcome of intensified relationships between men and plants rather than of any dramatic discovery or invention, something fully understandable in the light of the accurate knowledge of plants possessed by recent foragers and recorded by modern anthropologists. By comparison with much of the Old World animals contributed relatively little to the supply of food during Neothermal times in Mesoamerica. Only two species were domesticated, and those late in the sequence: dogs, although present rarely in the Abejas, were not plentiful until the Palo Blanco phase, and turkey first appeared during the Venta Salada phase in the Tehuacan valley. A final point to make about the Tehuacan sequence of particular interest to Old World prehistorians is that pottery first appeared in the Purrón phase (MacNeish *et al.* 1967, 11), that is at least five thousand years after undoubted evidence for plant domestication. It is hardly surprising, when we reflect that during the preceding phases cultivated plants still played a role subsidiary to wild ones, that the inhabitants of Tehuacan should have remained content with the non-ceramic receptacles such as gourds and baskets that sufficed for plant foods obtained by foraging. Again, it is probably no coincidence that pottery first came into use precisely at the same time that domesticated plants began to predominate over wild ones as sources of food. Thus, agriculture was practised before pottery was made in the New World as well as in the Old.

New thinking on the evolution of systems of food procurement during the early Neothermal phase both in Europe and south-west Asia also points in the same direction. Eric Higgs and his team, working on the British Academy Early History of Agriculture Project (1967–77) at Cambridge, laid consistent emphasis on the need to interpret animal and plant remains from archaeological sites in economic terms and specifically in terms of relationships that changed over time (Higgs 1972, 1974; Jarman 1977). They laid particular stress on the fact that the morphological criteria by which biologists determined whether remains of animals or plants related to 'wild' or 'domestic' species could only be expected to appear when relationships were sufficiently advanced to result in genetic change. In other words, they maintained that the morphological criteria in common use and embedded in the literature related not to 'domestication' as such but rather to a particular phase in this long drawn-out process (Brothwell 1975). The idea that domestication was a gradual process rather than a sudden innovation and was the outcome of changed sets of relationships was, of course, by no means invented by the Cambridge group. Dexter Perkins' analysis of sheep bones from intermediate levels at Shanidar, Iraq, had already shown a clear appreciation of the possibility of detecting early phases in the process by statistical rather than morphological means (Perkins 1964, cf. Chaplin 1969). Domestication might be expected in such terms to have been both gradual and likely to have occurred wherever circumstances were propitious. It could hardly have been abrupt and is most unlikely to have been unique.

NORTH-EAST IRAQ : KURDISTAN

In planning field operations, Braidwood worked on the principle that economic systems and more particularly prehistoric subsistence economies can only be understood in relation to total ecosystems. This led him to insist on working with inter-disciplinary teams and it also guided him in his choice of terrain for intensive survey. He realised that in seeking to fill his 'gap' nothing was to be gained by digging ever deeper into the alluvial plains that supported the rise of the earliest cities and states. Instead he realised that his best hope was to explore the uplands bordering Breasted's 'Fertile Crescent'. In this he was supported by the fact that even in the Assyrian zone of dry

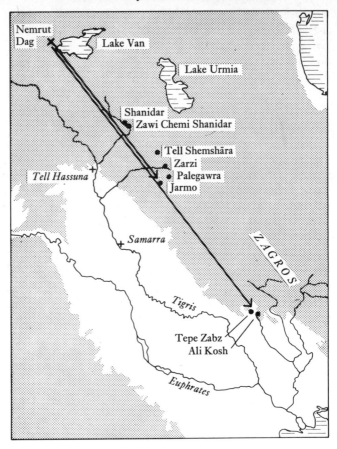

Figure 3. Map of key transitional sites in north-east Iraq
and south-west Iran, showing the extent of the obsidian
redistribution network from the Nemrut Dag source.
(Screening indicates land over 200 m)

farming, excavators had already dug very deep without finding
preceramic occupation. It seemed logical to move closer to the
upland regions where traces of terminal hunters had already
been located and into the piedmont zone where wild prototypes
of cultivated cereals were known to exist (figure 3).

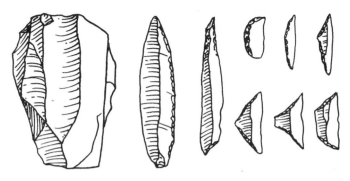

Figure 4. Lithic industry from Palegawra, north-east Iraq.

One of the first tasks was to verify and if possible amplify knowledge of the terminal hunter-gatherers who stood so to say on the threshold of the 'gap'. Bruce Howe's excavations in the rock-shelter of Palegawra (Braidwood and Howe 1960, 28f and 57ff) brought to light a flint industry (figure 4) closely parallel to that from the upper zone of Miss Garrod's Zarzian level and including geometric microliths, triangles, trapezes and, less commonly, lunates. The inhabitants of the Palegawra cave exploited a wide variety of animal resources including gazelle, wild goat, sheep (probably wild), a large bovid, an equid (probably an onager), red deer and pig (Turnbull 1974). A similar assemblage was found in the lower part (B2) of the penultimate deposit in the cave of Shanidar excavated by Ralph Solecki (1963), dated to 10050 ± 400 B.C. (W-179) in terms of radiocarbon. The upper zone of the same deposit (B1) which gave a consistent radiocarbon date (W-667, 8650 ± 300 B.C.), yielded presumptive evidence for a relationship between men and goats tantamount to an early phase of domestication. Indeed, as we have seen it was Dexter Perkins' analysis of this particular material that first suggested the possibility of detecting a phase in the process of domestication during which in his own words, 'the domestic form was identical morphologically with the wild'. Analysis of the age and sex composition of the goat population revealed an absence of very old animals and a predominance of immature ones, more particularly of males. The readiest explanation for such a composition is that it reflects human selection and herd management.

Another landmark in the prehistory of Kurdistan was the appearance of villages at a time before pottery had come into use. One of the oldest of these so far reported (w-681, 8850± 300 B.C.), Zawi Chemi Shanidar (Solecki 1964), was situated near the banks of the Greater Zab only a few miles from the rock shelter. The presence of three building phases and evidence for cultural change in the course of its history argues for a settlement of some duration. The economy differed from that previously encountered in that, to judge from the quantity of rubbing and pounding equipment made from pecked and polished stone, plant food was more important. Second, the rise to predominance of sheep in the upper part of the deposit and the high proportion of bones of immature individuals suggests domesticated herds. The flint industry continued throughout to maintain an ultimately Zarzian tradition, and a crescentic bone handle slotted or grooved along its concave edge to receive microblades merits particular attention. The upper levels were marked by the appearance of polished stone celts, but still yielded no pottery.

In many ways the most impressive, though as yet only summarily published (Braidwood and Howe 1960), excavations in the preceramic levels of an established village settlement are those carried out at the site of Jarmo by Robert and Linda Braidwood since 1948 on behalf of the Oriental Institute of Chicago. Allowing for erosion, the mound would have covered an area of more than four acres, and at least twelve building levels were visible in rather over seven metres of accumulated deposit. The houses forming the village were built of mud (*tauf*) on stone pebble foundations and contained a number of small compartments, some of them perhaps bins for storage. They were also provided with clay ovens and doors that swung on pivot stones. The villagers used a lithic industry made from flint and obsidian (figure 5). The important thing to note is that this was based on blades and microliths which

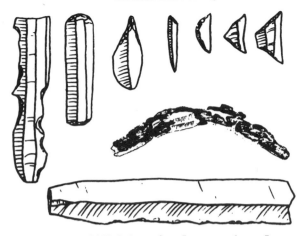

Figure 5. Lithic industry from Jarmo, north-east Iraq.

consistently predominated over larger tools at all levels. The microliths themselves compared closely with those from the Palegawra cave, including such geometric forms as triangles, trapezes and, in lesser numbers, lunates or crescents. End-scrapers and awls were also common, and large numbers of blades were adapted to form the cutting edges of sickles or reaping knives. Although no actual hafts were recovered from this site, some of the sickle blades still bore traces of the bitumen that served to hold them firm in their grooves.

A further indication of the importance of plant food and more particularly of cereals is given by the occurrence of milling and pounding equipment of ground stone. Other artefacts of ground stone included celts and a wide range of personal ornaments from bracelets to beads and pendants. A feature particularly noted by the excavators was the complete absence of pottery from the lower two-thirds or so of the deposit. This can hardly be explained in terms of differential conservation, since coarse pottery survived in the upper third and clay figurines of animals and people occurred down to the bottom (Braidwood and Howe 1960, 44). It is possible that the early inhabitants of Jarmo made extensive use of wooden containers as we know was the case at Çatal Hüyük in Anatolia (Mellaart 1967, fig.55). It is certain that they wove mats and twined baskets which they sometimes rendered waterproof by lining with bitumen. The pottery from the upper levels at Jarmo has been compared with the coarser wares of Hassunan age. This seems to be confirmed by the Danish excavations at Tell Shemshāra (Mortensen 1962, 76ff) on the Lesser Zab further north, where three levels lacking pottery and with a lithic industry closely resembling that from Jarmo with sickle-blades, and scrapers, awls and microliths, predominantly of obsidian and associated with grooved bone hafts, polished celts and a wealth of grinding and pounding equipment, was over-laid by a sequence of deposits containing pottery of Hassunan-Samarran styles. It looks as though we are justified in terming the Jarmo levels not merely aceramic but, at least locally speaking, preceramic. So far as it goes this is confirmed by the evidence of radiocarbon dating, since in conventional terms Braidwood's best estimate is *c.* 6750 B.C. for the attainment of the Jarmo level, a thousand years earlier than that of the Hassunan (Braidwood 1973, 316).

The archaeological evidence greatly enhances the importance of the associated biological residues. Charles Reed's study of the animal bones (Braidwood and Howe 1960, ch.IX) indicates that the Jarmo people preyed on a wide range of herbivorous species, including gazelle, red and roe deer, an equid (probably onager), a bovid, pig, sheep and goat. The only animals to show morphological evidence for genetic change were goats, which showed a tendency towards a flatten-ing of the horn core. Examination of plant residues indicate that pistachio nuts and acorns were still harvested, but wheat and barley were at least main sources of plant food (figure 6). In summarising the conclusions he drew from his examination of the cereal evidence – and it must be remembered that he was writing twenty years ago – Hans Helbaek commented (Braid-wood and Howe 1960, 102f) that:

> at Jarmo we are faced with the earliest stage of plant husbandry yet discovered. . . . However, that even Jarmo

does not represent the very first steps in the agricultural economy is suggested by the fact that its wheat spikelets seem to belong to a crop of conspicuously mixed character, some of them being large and coarse, others more delicate and bearing more resemblance to the typical cultivated emmer.

Figure 6. Seventh-millennium B.C. cereals from Jarmo, north-east Iraq: (*left*) cast of imprint of spikelet of emmer wheat (*Triticum dicoccoides*), and (*right*) carbonised kernels of two-row barley (*Hordeum distichum*).

SOUTH-WEST IRAN : LURISTAN AND KHUZISTAN

The successful outcome of American expeditions to Iraqi Kurdistan encouraged prehistorians from many countries, including Canada, Denmark, France, Japan and the United Kingdom as well as the United States, to extend exploration further east and south along the piedmont zone of the Zagros mountain range. No attempt will be made here to describe in a comprehensive manner the rich discoveries made with the beneficient co-operation of the Iranian authorities. Instead, attention will be concentrated on a particular series of investigations, aimed specifically at elucidating the process by which terminal hunting groups gave place to fully achieved village communities, those conducted by Frank Hole, Kent Flannery and their associates in the mountainous territory of Luristan and on the Deh Luran plain of adjacent Khuzistan (Hole and Flannery 1967; Hole, Flannery and Neely 1969).

Although gaps have still to be filled before the case can be proved, it looks as though the precursors of the Khuzistan villages had originally been based on the caves and rock-shelters of Luristan. The flint industries from the earliest villages included fluted cores and microliths, and it is significant that the latter, modified by changes of pattern, persisted into the fourth millennium B.C. On the other hand, the blades of sickles (or more correctly reaping knives) were already present in the earliest village levels. Analysis of organic traces from successive levels shows that subsistence underwent gradual but progressive changes (figure 7). Whereas dry farming was at first subsidiary to hunting and gathering, it came in due course to replace these activities as the principle source of food. Again, the productivity of agriculture was greatly enhanced by the development of effective irrigation. By far the most important source of meat during the dry farming phase was that furnished by caprines, in itself a sign of movement from the highlands to the steppe plains. Among the caprines sheep were markedly subsidiary to goats. The predominance of young males and the complete absence of old individuals among the caprines argues for some degree of domestication from the beginning, though signs of genetic change did not appear until the Ali Kosh phase. Gazelle and onager were fairly strongly represented to begin with, but their noteworthy decline from the Sabz phase onwards argues against them having been domesticated.

The plant record is particularly informative. Remains from

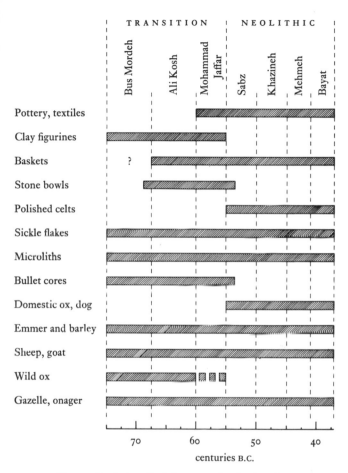

Figure 7. Evolution of subsistence and technology in Khuzistan, 7500-3700 B.C. (after Hole and Flannery).

the Bus Mordeh phase suggest that the earliest villagers confronted a steppe environment. Some 90 per cent of the seeds recovered comprised those of wild legumes, among which wild alfalfa, spiny vetch (*Astragalus*) and a small number of the pea family (*Trigonella*) had evidently been systematically harvested, as well as wild grasses, including oats. By contrast cultivated cereals, which included emmer wheat and two-rowed hulled barley, accounted for less than 10 per cent in number though not, of course, in volume. By Ali Kosh times there was already a dramatic increase in the proportion of cultivated cereals to 40 per cent. By Mohammad Jaffar times, when sheep were gaining rapidly on goats, fallowing and grazing had so greatly modified the former steppe vegetation that pasture plants like plantain, vetch, mallow and grasses were prominent alongside cultivated cereals.

The Sabz phase was marked by many developments. The beginnings of irrigation on a substantial scale inaugurated a new phase in subsistence, reflected both in livestock and in crops. Domestic ox and dog appeared, sheep increased dramatically at the expense of goat and both gazelle and onager declined. In respect of crops there was a notable increase in the size of flax seeds (Helbaek 1960) and the range of cultivated plants was enlarged by the addition of hexaploid wheat and six-row barley. Pottery underwent a marked technical improvement, harder wares being produced at higher temperatures. At this time also polished stone celts appeared to complete the inventory of traits specified by Lubbock as defining the Neolithic. Incomplete though the evidence remains, the general trend is evident. The inhabitants of south-west Iran, like those of Kurdistan, Palestine or for that matter of Mexico or Peru, can be seen to have modified both their environment and their biological and technical resources gradually and almost insensibly, and certainly not in any sudden or revolutionary manner. There was continuity of development from a state of affairs characterised by Old World prehistorians as Upper Palaeolithic to one which for over a hundred years they have agreed to call Neolithic. In terms of Kurdistan and the Zagros the Mesolithic can be seen as a phase of the utmost importance in the unfolding of prehistory. It was a period in which were wrought those momentous changes that made possible the attainment of the earliest civilisations of man.

PALESTINE AND JORDAN

Thanks to their exploration by prehistoric archaeologists during the last half century (for a useful summary see Perrot 1968), Palestine and Jordan have each contributed notably to our understanding of the transition from economies based solely on hunting and gathering to ones in which farming played a predominant role (figure 8). The joint expedition mounted between 1929–34 by the British School of Archaeology in Jerusalem and the American School of Prehistoric Research, under the direction of Miss Dorothy Garrod, focused on the Wadi el-Mughara on the western side of Mount Carmel (Garrod and Bate 1937). Each of the caves excavated revealed Middle Palaeolithic deposits, and at both et-Tabūn and es-Skhūl these contained Neanderthal burials. On the other hand, the most important in the present context was el-Wad. Here no less than four phases of Upper Palaeolithic occupation overlay the Middle Palaeolithic and were themselves capped by assemblages which Miss Garrod was quick to categorise as Mesolithic. These were named as Natufian after the Wadi en-Natuf where was situated the Shukbah cave in which they were first found in a stratified deposit (Garrod and Bate 1942). As has become increasingly evident, the Natufian has provided a significant clue to an understanding of the process by which the transition from Palaeolithic to Neolithic was accomplished in this part of south-western Asia.

Although in common with other Mesolithic assemblages the Natufian displayed many Upper Palaeolithic traits, notably blades, burins, steep blunting retouch and the use of antler and bone for a variety of artefacts, it was distinguished by an exceptionally high proportion of microliths, amounting in level B1 to 80 per cent and in level B2 to 77 per cent of recorded implements and by the occurrence of such specialised traits as slotted or grooved hafts and fish hooks. It was also marked by a complete absence of the traits most widely associated with the Neolithic, including pottery, polished flint axes and the bones of animals showing genetic modifications indicative of an

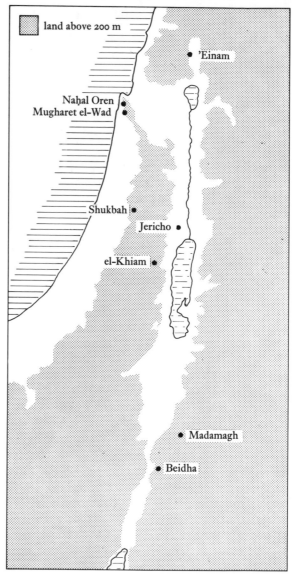

Figure 8. Map of key transitional sites in Palestine and Jordan.

advanced stage in domestication. Although she was at first inclined to identify the newly found microlithic industry as Capsian, closer study soon led Miss Garrod to the opinion that what she had found was no mere extension from north Africa but a new and original manifestation of Mesolithic culture. The lunate microliths that formed so predominant a feature of the industry were distinguished in many cases by the fact that the blunting of the backs had been achieved by steep flaking from two directions. This bipolar flaking and the general composition of the industry made Natufian assemblages easy to identify. It is now evident that although concentrated most densely in Palestine between the Rift Valley and the Mediterranean, the Natufian extended north to Syria and south to Jordan, Sinai and the Nile delta.

The Natufian is thus a markedly local culture and if, as we may suppose, it stemmed from Upper Palaeolithic sources, it is reasonable to seek to identify these within its own territory. Evidence is most likely to come from cave sequences. It is, however, important to reckon with the fact that even the most advantageous caves are likely to have been settled only intermittently. We cannot expect, therefore, to find Natufian levels invariably, or necessarily ever, stratified directly above their immediate Upper Palaeolithic antecedents. At the original site, Shukbah, indeed, the Natufian directly overlay a Middle Palaeolithic deposit and at el-Wad itself it rested on one containing an Upper Palaeolithic 5 (Atlitian) industry. At the time of her Reckitt Lecture Professor Garrod was still fully justified in commenting that the Natufian appeared to make 'its first appearance apparently full-grown with no traceable roots in the past' (Garrod 1957, 212). Not even the Upper Palaeolithic 6 (Kebaran) industry underlying the Natufian level in the el-Kebarah cave has provided any clear indication. It was the recent excavations at Naḥal Ōren on the coastal side of Mount Carmel, only a short distance north of the Wadi el-Mughara, that yielded for the first time a plausible prototype for the Natufian in a notably microlithic version of the Kebaran (Noy, Legge and Higgs 1973). Even the flints from the bottom layer (level IX) were sensibly more microlithic than the Kebaran industry from the eponymous site. The microlithic trend was even more marked in level VII, which yielded geometrical forms including some crescents but predominantly triangles. By comparison the immediately overlying Natufian was marked by a replacement of triangles by crescents as the dominant form. It looks, even in the present defective state of knowledge, as if there was a genuine continuity between the Natufian and the microlithic phase of the Kebaran tradition.

The discovery of a geometric phase of the Kebaran in stratigraphic position between the underlying classical phase and the overlying Natufian offers a strong presumption of cultural continuity. To prove the case would require fine microstratigraphic studies of cave or shelter deposits controlled by close radiocarbon dating. In the meantime existing radiocarbon determinations serve to define the gap. Determinations from non-geometric Kebaran levels at Naḥal Ōren (layer IX, UCLA-1776C: 18250±320 BP) and at Rakefet (1.6865: 18910± 300 BP) suggest that this phase of Palestinian prehistory began at least as early as 17000 B.C. Consistent with these determinations are two samples taken from a geometric Kebaran level at Naḥal Ōren (UCLA-1776A: 15800±300 BP and 1776B: 16880±340 BP) suggesting that this phase was flourishing around 14000 B.C. still leaving a considerable gap in time before the earliest date generally accepted for the beginning of the Natufian (*c.* 10000 B.C.). Too much significance should not on the other hand be attached to this. By contrast with northern Europe where the onset of Neothermal climate can be precisely dated, no comparable change has been demonstrated in the Levant to define the end of the Pleistocene. The crucial point to note is the absence of any clear break in environment, technology or, as we shall see, economy.

It has still been possible for prehistorians to observe a succession of stratigraphic phases (figure 9). To take first the evidence from caves and rock-shelters, Miss Garrod noted a clear division in her Natufian phase: whereas level B2 contained a Lower Natufian defined by a notably larger proportion

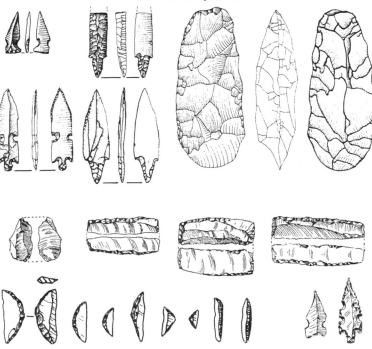

Figure 9. Natufian (*below*) and Tahunian (*above*)
lithic industries.

(58.75 per cent) of lunate microliths with bipolar retouch,
level BI produced an Upper Natufian with a markedly lower
proportion (24.63 per cent). Neuville (1951) extended the
sequence by recovering a distinctive Tahunian assemblage,
named after its first occurrence in the Ouady Tahounah
(Buzy 1928) and marked by pressure-flaked arrowheads
mainly tanged in form (Perrot 1952) and axes and picks
sharpened by the tranchet technique, immediately overlying
an Upper Natufian layer. He further claimed to distinguish
two phases in the Upper Natufian itself, an earlier one with
lunates having a characteristically low proportion of bipolar
flaking (14 per cent) and a later one marked by el-Khiam arrowheads with square bases and side-notches, a form of which only

isolated examples occurred in the Upper Natufian at the el-Wad.

Dr (later Dame) Kathleen Kenyon's excavations at Tell es-Sultan, Jericho, opened up a new dimension in the study of the transitional phase of the Stone Age in the Levant. Jericho provided the first parallel in this region to Braidwood's crucial discovery at Jarmo, N. Iraq (see p.18). It confirmed that settled life based to some extent on farming and resulting in the formation of tells had been initiated by people who had not yet begun to make pottery. From a stratigraphical standpoint Jericho was indeed more informative than Jarmo. Not only could two levels, distinguished by architecture and the incidence of certain lithic types, be detected in the so-called 'Pre-pottery Neolithic' (PPN),[2] but these were themselves preceded by an initial phase of settlement marked by an enigmatic structural feature, possibly some kind of shrine, and by a lithic assemblage of lower Natufian character. The settlement of Tell es-Sultan, focused on the spring by which the Natufians encamped, appeared to the excavator to have been occupied continuously from the Lower Natufian into the PPN (table 1). To quote (the italics are mine) from Dr Kenyon (1959):

> From this Mesolithic structure, sanctuary or whatever it may be, the succession to the Pre-pottery Neolithic A town is unbroken. The analysis of the flint and bone industries is not yet complete, *but it is already clear that they are essentially Natufian throughout*.

It follows, as Dr Kenyon recognised in the same article, that during its transitional phases the stone age of Palestine and Jordan followed two parallel lines of development; one reflected by the cave and shelter sequences, the other docu-

2. The term 'Pre-pottery Neolithic' is self-contradictory in the light of Lubbock's very clear definition of the Neolithic as including, along with other qualifications, the making of pottery. In the present text the letters PPN will be used as a guide to texts in which the term has been employed. Although Braidwood was the first to open up non-ceramic deposits containing evidence for what he termed 'incipient farming', he avoided referring to them as 'Pre-pottery Neolithic'.

Table 1. Sequence of levels at key sites marking the
Palaeolithic-Neolithic transition in Palestine and Jordan.

Approx. C14 dates B.C.	Period	Caves and Rock-shelters			Open Settlements	
		el-Wad (Garrod)	el-Khiam (Neuville)	Naḥal Ōren (Noy, Legge, Higgs)	Jericho (Kenyon)	Beidha (Mortensen)
5000	NEO 2				PN B	
6000	NEO 1				PN A	
7000	MESO 3 (Tahunian)		A (Tahunian)	I–II	PPN B	I–III
8500	MESO 2	BI (Upper Natufian)	BI B2	III–IV	PPN A	IV–IX
10000	MESO 1	B2 (Lower Nat.)	C (Sterile)	V–VI	MESO (Lower Nat.)	X
17000	U.PAL 6		D (Kebaran)	VII–IX		
	U.PAL 5	C (Atlitian)	E			

mented in the open settlements occupied by groups that had
come to exercise a greater measure of control over their
resources of food. Evidence for synchronising the two
sequences, apart from radiocarbon chronology, may be cited
from Beidha in south Jordan and from Naḥal Ōren, Mount
Carmel, the material from which has been carefully analysed
from a stratigraphic point of view. At Beidha the initial occupation was of Lower Natufian character (Kirkbride 1966), as at
Jericho, and the PPN villages showed the same broad succession
of curvilinear houses followed by rectangular structures with
plastered walls and floors (figure 10). Similarly, despite some
differentiation in successive layers, notably the appearance in
PPN B of Tahunian tanged arrowheads with flat flaking and
axes and picks with tranchet edges, Mortensen's seriation
study (1970) of the flint types demonstrated a degree of

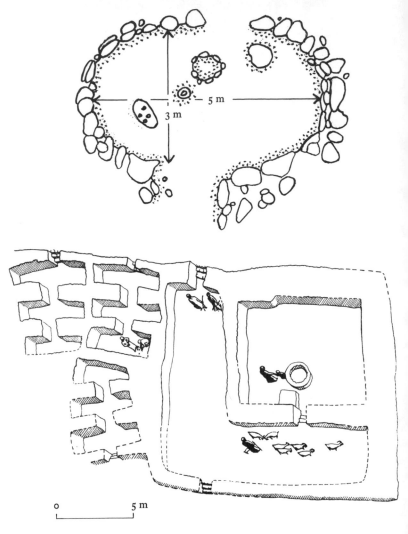

Figure 10. Round and oblong house plans of the transitional phase in Palestine: (*above*) rounded plan from PPN A level at Naḥal Ōren (after Stekelis and Yizraely), and (*below*) plans of oblong structures with plaster floors from PPN B level at Beidha (after Kirkbride).

continuity that argued for the persistence of the same ethnic group throughout.

The most direct evidence for food procurement comprises biological traces of animals and plants from early settlements. It is unfortunate that until archaeologists concerned themselves with reconstructing the economic basis of early communities they failed to take systematic samples of such materials. Even so sufficient evidence has been recorded from modern excavations, some undertaken for this special purpose, to provide a broad outline of the sequence from the closing Kebaran phase of the Upper Palaeolithic to the beginning of the Neolithic in the sense defined by Lubbock. A point that may be stressed first of all is that even in a region as small as Palestine and Jordan climatic, topographic and biological circumstances varied during prehistoric times, as they still do, from one territory to another. During the final Upper Palaeolithic, and throughout the period of transition, gazelle accounted for threequarters or more of the kill in the Mount Carmel region, whereas in south Jordan goat occupied the same position (figure 11). One of the few notable changes in time occurred in the Naḥal Ōren sequence, in which goat appeared in the PPN A level and rose in PPN B to about one-seventh of the total. It has been argued (Legge 1972), on account of the high proportion of young animals represented among the goat remains from Natufian and PPN levels (75 and 54.5 per cent) at Beidha, that these animals were subject to some form of cultural control on the way to domestication, in contrast with the situation in the Kebaran level at the nearby Madamagh shelter where the proportion was only 23.1 per cent (Kirkbride 1958).

Another line of approach, catchment analysis of the kind carried out by Higgs and Vita-Finzi (Vita-Finzi and Higgs 1970) for a number of key sites, including the Wadi el-Mughara and Jericho, has proved of value in defining the options open to prehistoric man. In the case of el-Wad, for example, half the territory within a 5-km radius comprised dunes and marshlands only seasonally attractive to grazing animals. On the assumption that the inhabitants depended in the main on a

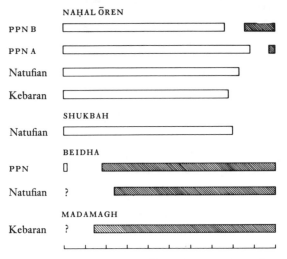

Figure 11. Histograms illustrating proportions of goat (*hatched bars*) and gazelle (*open bars*) from sites in the coastal zone (Naḥal Ōren and Shukbah) and inland zone (Beidha and Madamagh) of Palestine and Jordan from the Upper Palaeolithic to the Mesolithic 3 (PPN B) phase.

meat diet it was argued that the remaining half of the territory would have been insufficient to maintain a group all the year round. It was envisaged that the hunters at least engaged in seasonal movements, following the herds as they moved between the interior uplands and the marshlands of the coastal zone that during the driest part of the year might have been valued for their reserves of moisture. This picture is slightly modified if it is assumed that advantage was in reality taken of the more certain and economic source of food embodied in plants. It is a notable fact that *c.* 17 per cent of the el-Wad territory consists of arable or potentially arable grazing. Again, between 8 and 9 per cent of the finished lithic artefacts from Natufian levels at el-Wad were the flint blades of reaping knives. Also stone mortars and pestles are a common component of Natufian assemblages. If the Natufians harvested wild cereals, even if they cultivated cereals, this does not preclude transhumance, particularly if we envisage that women and children remained at permanent homes. No traces of plant food are available from the Natufian levels at el-Wad, Beidha or Jericho, and it is a fact that no traces of cultivated cereal were present in the small sample from Naḥal Ōren.[3] On the other hand, the rich discoveries made at Beidha (Helbaek 1966) in a deposit immediately overlying the Natufian are particularly worthy of note since they took the form of impressions on clay from the floor and roof of a particular house (E130) at a low level in the PPN A village. These included tens of thousands of imprints of barley corresponding to the wild prototype (*Hordeum spontaneum*) except that the grains were larger, indicating most probably an initial phase in the process of domestication. Emmer, while appearing entirely in its domesticated form (*Triticum dicoccum*), displayed a high degree of variability of a kind characteristic of plants in the process of genetic transition. Although the sample from the PPN A level at Jericho was too small to be of statistical value, it included wheat and barley (Hopf 1969). Further, as at Beidha, einkorn, the wild prototype of which was not certainly present in this territory, was absent and did not appear until the PPN B occupation. The earliest villagers in Beidha certainly harvested wild pistachio nuts (*P. atlantica*) and probably acorns, both prolific crops still harvested and eaten by the local nomads.

SUMMARY

The picture revealed by intensive research in territories at either end of the 'Fertile Crescent' is broadly similar. In each the 'gap' defined by the Oriental Institute of Chicago, equivalent to the 'hiatus' of late nineteenth-century prehistorians, has been found to be illusory. Excavation assisted by radiocarbon dating, another contribution from Chicago, this time from the

3. Three grains of wheat (*T. dicoccum*) and one of barley (*Hordeum*) were recovered from a Kebaran level at Naḥal Ōren (Noy, Legge and Higgs 1973, 92f). One cannot discount the possibility that these grains were introduced by burrowing rodents and it would probably be best to await confirmatory finds before drawing wide-ranging conclusions.

Institute of Nuclear Physics,[4] has demonstrated or at least rendered acceptable as a working hypothesis that there was a substantial degree of continuity between the last full-scale hunter-foragers in this region and the earliest communities to depend largely on farming. Although many key sites were investigated before modern methods of securing adequate samples of food residues had been devised,[5] and before recent thinking on the reconstruction of early systems of food procurement had been carried out, it is already evident that the change from exploitive to productive economies was as gradual in the Old World as it has also been shown to have been in the New (see pp.11–14). By the same token stratigraphic studies aided by radiocarbon dating, although still incomplete, have already suggested that, whether in Kurdistan, the Zagros or Palestine and Jordan, cultural traditions, although undergoing modifications in the course of time, were remarkably persistent. In brief, modern research has shown that ethnic groups underwent gradual but cumulatively substantial changes in both subsistence and technology. In Old World terminology the transition from a Palaeolithic to a Neolithic stage as defined by Lubbock was accomplished by men of an intermediate or Mesolithic age, men moreover whose technology compared in many ways with that already known from Mesolithic Europe. It was Mesolithic communities who were responsible for laying the economic basis for the rise of the earliest cities and ultimately of the earliest states with communications systems that included writing and the possibility of recorded history.

4. Libby, Anderson and Arnold (1949) specifically acknowledged help from the Department of Anthropology at the University of Chicago in the first announcement of the age determination of archaeological samples by radiocarbon dating.
5. The difference between the recovery rates from visual inspection and sieving has been particularly well brought out in respect of lithic material, pottery and animal bones by S. Payne (1972). In respect of plant residues attention may be drawn to Jarman, Legge and Charles (1972).

Table 2. The transition from communities based exclusively on hunting and foraging to those based substantially on farming in zones of south-west Asia.

.C.	Period	Economies	Palestine-Jordan	N.W. Iraq	S.W. Iran
000		Pottery-using	PN B	Hassuna–	
	NEOLITHIC	Stone Age	PN A	Samarra	Sabz
000		farmers			M. Jaffar
000			PPN B/Tahunian	Jarmo	Ali Kosh
000		Transition to	PPN A/Upper Natufian		Bus Mordeh
	MESOLITHIC	basic farming		Zawi Chemi	
000		economy	Lower Natufian	Shanidar	
0000			(gap)	Zarzian	
7000	UPPER PALAEO-	Hunting, fishing, fowling and	Kebaran	(gap)	
9000	LITHIC	foraging the	Atlitian		
		exclusive base		Baradostian	
3000					

37

3

MESOLITHIC
SETTLEMENT IN
EUROPE

INTRODUCTION

If the Mesolithic was an age of crucial innovation in parts of
south-west Asia, what was going forward during early Neothermal times in the continent that provided the first discoveries and in which the very concept was formed? On a
superficial view the archaeological discoveries, on which Miles
Burkitt raised his pupils at Cambridge half a century ago and in
terms of which I myself sought to define a new age of British
prehistory, were sufficiently meagre to account for the dim,
even apologetic image of what is now widely recognised, in the
light of research in south-west Asia and in many parts of
Europe, to have been a crucial period in prehistory. It soon
became evident that the most promising way of gaining an
adequate picture of the achievements of the inhabitants of
Europe between the end of the Ice Age and the adoption of a
Neolithic way of life was to adopt an ecological approach and
deploy the full armoury of Quaternary Research. One reason
why the territories of the west Baltic area offered the best
opportunities in this regard is that it was precisely in the former
periglacial zone that the transition from Late-glacial to Neothermal conditions was most sharply defined (summarised in
Clark 1936, Nordmann 1936, Brøndsted 1938, Schwantes
1939). It was the inhabitants of this region who had for this
reason to make the most radical adjustments to adapt to the
new conditions, just as it was there that geological deposits dis-

38

played the most clearly defined sequence of geographical, climatic and biological change. By the same token it was here that scientists responded most inventively by developing techniques like pollen analysis and evolving methods of work best suited to working out the context of human settlement in their correct ecological contexts. In addition to all this the region provided exceptional conditions for the survival of organic substances. This in turn meant that a much wider range of artefacts was commonly available for study, as well as animal bones and vegetable remains capable of giving a clear insight into the systems of food-procurement practised at different periods.

In view of this it is hardly surprising that most of the information on which estimates of the achievements of Meso-lithic man in Europe depend comes from the northern parts of the temperate zone (Clark 1975). On the other hand, the expansion of pollen analysis over much of western and central Europe and the widespread application of radiocarbon dating now makes it possible to correlate the northern cultural sequence with that in other parts of Europe (table 3).

In historical terms it is true enough that at a time when Late-glacial conditions were giving way to Neothermal, the inhabit-ants of different parts of Europe were Epipalaeolithic in the sense that they owed much of their initial culture to their Upper Palaeolithic forebears. This is well documented in their technology, as well as in their general mode of subsistence and, particularly in territories provided with caves and rock-shelters, in their choice of locations of settlement. In flint work the use of burins and of the steep retouch for backing bladelets are among the most noteworthy Upper Palaeolithic traits featured in Mesolithic industries. In antler and bone work the use of the groove and splinter technique for extracting blanks (Clark and Thompson 1953) was a feature of the Azilian industries of north Spain and the French Pyrenees, of the Maglemosian and Proto-maglemosian of northern Europe and of the late Mesolithic Fürstein industry of the Alpine Foreland (Wyss 1968, Abb.14 no.24).

39

Table 3. West European settlement between *c.* 2500 and 10000 B.C.

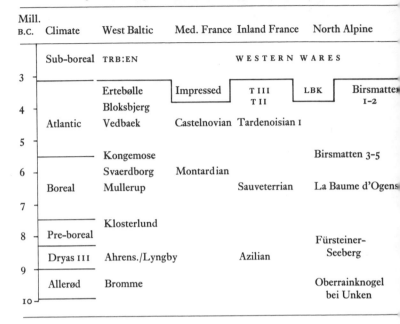

Mill. B.C.	Climate	West Baltic	Med. France	Inland France	North Alpine	
	Sub-boreal	TRB:EN		WESTERN WARES		
3		Ertebølle	Impressed	T III	LBK	Birsmatter
4		Bloksbjerg		T II		1-2
	Atlantic	Vedbaek	Castelnovian	Tardenoisian I		
5						
		Kongemose			Birsmatten 3-5	
6		Svaerdborg	Montardian			
	Boreal	Mullerup		Sauveterrian	La Baume d'Ogens	
7						
		Klosterlund				
8	Pre-boreal				Fürsteiner-	
	Dryas III	Ahrens./Lyngby		Azilian	Seeberg	
9						
	Allerød	Bromme			Oberrainknogel bei Unken	
10						

Yet the more we learn about the people who occupied Europe between *c.* 8000 and 6000 B.C. the clearer it becomes that they were far from being mere survivors prolonging an earlier mode of life. Bioarchaeological studies have revealed how effectively they in fact adapted to environmental change, developed complex systems of food-procurement and devised material equipment admirably suited to their needs. In a word they fully earned the right to be termed Mesolithic, culturally as well as temporally, even in this territory remote from the main focus of innovation at this time in south-west Asia.

ECOLOGY AND TECHNOLOGY

Although when I first reviewed the evidence from northern Europe I laid particular emphasis on linking archaeological assemblages with their natural settings, I had yet to apply ecological theory to prehistory in any thorough-going way. Even in emphasising how some of the key features of the northern Mesolithic assemblages could best be understood as adaptations to changes in the physical environment I had two important predecessors. As long ago as 1923 Gustaf Schwantes had interpreted the hafted axe and adze as adaptations to the spread of forest at the beginning of Postglacial times (Schwantes 1923, 1928). Again, Gordon Childe (1931) had displayed his characteristic ambivalence towards the Mesolithic by contributing a brilliant paper on the cultural assemblages of Maglemose type that extended, during the mainland phase when the Baltic was a lake and much of the North Sea dry land, from eastern England as far east as Finland. He attributed the degree of community exhibited by these to the fact that they were all adapted to cope with the Postglacial forest.

One result of approaching the data from a more sophisticated ecological viewpoint[1] was further to underscore the need for interdisciplinary Quaternary research, both to synchronise phases in the development of habitat, biome and culture through more refined pollen analysis and systematic radiocarbon dating and to explore the reciprocal interaction between the components of ecosystems and various aspects of culture. This last may be illustrated by reference to the forests that expanded during Postglacial times over the whole of the north European plain, replacing the relatively open landscape of Late-glacial times and only stopping short at rivers, lakes, swamps and the immediate zones of coasts (Godwin 1956, 326f). The human population seems to have responded in a direct way by initiating the process of forest clearance that permitted, and in the long run was drastically accelerated by, the introduction of farming. The marked rise of hazel pollen in

1. The need to interpret archaeological evidence in terms of the societies that gave rise to it was a main theme of *Archaeology and Society* (Clark 1939). In my Reckitt Lecture of 1952 I enlarged the model of 1939 to include the habitats and biomes of the total ecosystems that comprehended human societies; see Clark (1953) especially pp.233ff. The same approach informed Clark (1952a) chapter 1, and on a local scale the investigations at Star Carr.

Late Boreal times, a shrub that spreads rapidly over ground cleared by burning, suggests that early man may have made his main impact on the forest by means of fire (Clark 1975, 53). While fire damage may well have occurred accidentally through its use in cooking and heating, wholesale burning under temperate conditions is more likely to have been intentional, whether as a tactic in hunting or conceivably as a means of improving grazing for animals like red deer. On the other hand Mesolithic man in this region undoubtedly felled timber and the stump of a birch tree from Star Carr (Clark *et al.* 1954, pl.IV) shows that he did so by cutting into the base of the trunk at an oblique angle (figure 12). For this and for shaping timber he made axes and adzes with flint blades by bifacial flaking, sharpened by removing transverse (*tranchet*) flakes and mounted in antler hafts designed to absorb some of the shock incurred in use (figure 13) and perforated to receive their wooden handles (Clark 1975, 53). In utilising wood he showed an evident appreciation of the qualities of different varieties (*ibid.*, 122–7). Thus elm and, as it became available with the rise of temperature, yew served for bow staves, pine for arrow shafts, hazel for spear shafts and tough root wood for axe hafts. The qualities of different types of bark were understood and exploited. The resistance of birch bark to water was seen to make it useful for insulating hut floors and making net floats and the pitch which made it burn so well was extracted for mounting the elements of composite artefacts, caulking containers and preparing leather (Clark *et al.*, 1954, 17 and 166f). Pine bark was seen to be well adapted for net floats and willow bark was made to yield the bast that served for the thread used for making nets. Not even such appendages of trees as bracket fungus (*Fomes fomentarius*) were overlooked and specimens from Star Carr were found to have been stripped of the outer skin traditionally used, down to recent times, for tinder (*ibid.*, 18; cf. Clark *et al.* 1950, 123f).

Figure 12. Birch trees felled in the mid–eighth
millennium B.C. uncovered at Star Carr, Yorkshire.

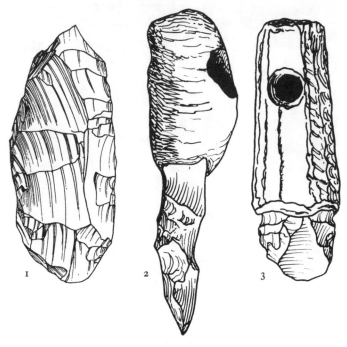

Figure 13. Mesolithic tree-felling and wood-working equipment from northern Europe: flint adze blade (1) and blades in wooden (2) and antler (3) hafts (approx. 2/3).

LAND ANIMALS

The replacement of an open by a forested landscape also greatly enlarged the range of animals available for meat. The earliest inhabitants of the west Baltic region had been able to satisfy many needs, skins for clothing and tents, sinews for sewing and binding, antler and bone for artefacts, and above all meat, from a single species, the highly gregarious reindeer that grazed the open landscape of the Late-glacial period (Clark 1952a, 22ff, and 1953, 220ff). The reindeer herds were all the more accessible in that their seasonal movements were largely predictable. The relationship was to a certain degree

44

symbiotic, for the reindeer also secured benefits. An enduring relationship implied a culling policy designed to secure the maximum return consistent with replenishment of the herds. Intelligent predation served to maintain the reindeer population at an optimum level having regard to grazing potential. In addition human predators protected the herds from a variety of casual carnivores as well as helping to maintain the quality of the breeding stock by eliminating sickly individuals (Sturdy 1975, 77). Yet one should avoid over-emphasising the degree of intimacy of the relationship between man and reindeer during the Late-glacial period. It would be going too far to rank it as tantamount to domestication. One of the most striking things to emerge from close scrutiny of the large quantities of reindeer skeletal remains from such a Late-glacial site as Stellmoor in Schleswig-Holstein is after all the evidence that reindeer were shot by flint-tipped arrows, something that would hardly have happened if the animals had been tamed (Rust 1943, pls.85–7).

If the rise of temperature and the spread of forest, not to mention the formation of many lakes from glacial melt-water and the gradual encroachment of the sea greatly enlarged the variety of food available to the inhabitants of the west Baltic area during early Postglacial times, it nevertheless required a high degree of adaptation and ingenuity to compensate for the loss of the reindeer herds. Animal remains recovered from Maglemosian sites show that aurochs, red deer and, for a time, elk were the main sources of meat, but that wild pig, roe deer and a variety of fur-bearing animals, as well as birds and fish also contributed their share (Clark 1975, app. C). Study of the animal material from a site like Star Carr suggests that the food quest was carefully scheduled on a seasonal basis, involving at least a degree of seasonal movement (Clark 1972a). Man/ animal relations involved, as they already had during the reindeer period, an attentive study of the habits and seasonal movements of prey, though now of a great variety of animals of different habits. On the other hand, although close relationships were a necessary preliminary to taming and full domestication, there is no evidence that red deer (Jarman 1972) or any other herbivore was in fact tamed in this context. Recent re-examination of the material from Star Carr by Nanna Nøe-Nygaard (1974) of Copenhagen has shown that the red deer skeletons, like those of reindeer from Stellmoor, displayed signs of wounds inflicted by man. Aurochs is another animal that was certainly hunted. Bones with wound marks have been recovered from several sites in Denmark and South Sweden and the well-known skeleton from Vig on Zealand had evidently been shot at on more than one occasion and by at least three arrows (Clark 1975, 137ff).

Since, as Wolf Heere (1969) was surely right to emphasise, the main reason for taming animals was to ensure more reliable supplies of meat, there was no particular motive for doing so when plenty was obtainable by hunting. The only animal domesticated in early Postglacial times in northern Europe was the dog, which to judge from its occurrence at Star Carr (Degerbøl 1961) had certainly been tamed from the wolf as early as the eighth millennium, that is well before it had been in south-west Asia (see p.24).

The most important weapon used for hunting in this terri-tory, and indeed over the whole of Europe, north Africa and south-west Asia, was the bow (Clark 1968), even if as a rule only the flint components of the arrows survived in the archaeo-logical record (figure 14). The first certain evidence for archery in the west Baltic area comes in the form of over a hundred arrowshafts from the ninth-millennium Ahrensburgian deposits at Stellmoor in Schleswig-Holstein. Their Hamburg-ian forerunners certainly used flint-headed projectiles, since these have been found embedded in reindeer skeletons, but it cannot yet be proved that these were propelled by bows. On the other hand, it is likely that the bow had been available to some groups in south-west Europe and parts of north Africa substantially earlier. At least, barbed and tanged flint points closely comparable in form and size with undoubted arrow-heads of much later date are known from Late Solutrean deposits at Parpalló in eastern Spain dating from *c.* 15000 B.C.

LAND ANIMALS

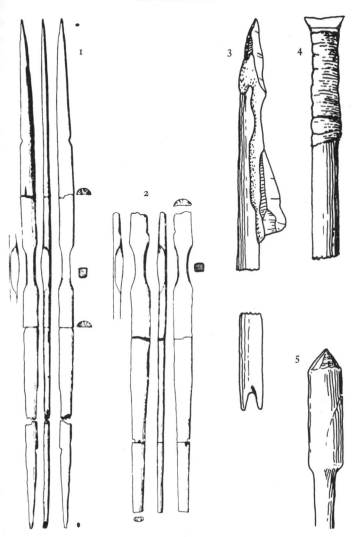

Figure 14. Evidence for Mesolithic archery from northern
Europe: (1, 2) bows from Holmegaard, Denmark (approx. 1/10);
(3) arrow with microlithic tip and barb from Loshult, Scania
(approx. 3/4); (4) cutting arrow from Eising, Jutland (approx.
3/4); (5) wooden bolt head from Holmegaard (approx. 3/4).

47

(Pericot 1942, fig.21). The earliest actual bows so far recovered were man-sized self-bows with shaped hand-grips and tapered limbs. The commonest form of flint arrowhead during the Late-glacial phase in northern Europe was the tanged point set in a cleft at the tip of the shaft as documented at Stellmoor. During Boreal times microliths made from sections of blades or bladelets were the most prominent component of lithic industries. Some like the minute triangles and crescents in the Sauveterrian industries of France (Coulanges 1935)[2] or that of La Baume d'Ogens in the Alpine Foreland[3] may have served as barbs for wooden spearheads. More or less symmetrical triangular points with square or concave bases may similarly have served to tip arrows. One of the few certainties is that triangular microliths were sometimes used to tip arrows: one was found embedded in the vertebra of one of the burials in the cemetery at Téviec in Morbihan (Péquart *et al.* 1937), and still more convincingly, another was discovered, still mounted in resin, at the tip of one of the arrowshafts recovered from Loshult, Scania (Petersson 1951). Another feature of the Loshult arrow is that two additional microliths, simple obliquely blunted points, were set in resin on one side of the head of the shaft with the cutting edge outermost. The effect of this was that a single arrow combined a cutting with a perforating function. In the final phase of the Mesolithic the perforating role appears to have given place in large measure and in some cases entirely to the cutting role in the design of arrows. The fashion spread of mounting rhombic and later exclusively trapeziform sections of blades at the tips of arrows in such a way as to present sharp chisel-like edges obliquely or trans-

2. The following radiocarbon dates (quoted B.C.) from Sauveterrian levels at Rouffignac appear to span the chronological range of the culture: GrN-2889, 5850±50; 2913, 6420±100; 2895, 6640±95; 2280, 7045±105; 5513, 6800±75; 5514, 7200±90.
3. E.g. at La Baume d'Ogens, Vaud, Switzerland, dating from the second quarter of the seventh millennium B.C. (B-765, 6785±150 and B-764, 6580±100; see Egloff and Oeschger *et al.* 1970). This compares with the industry from level C in the rock-shelter of Zigeunerfels, near Sigmaringen, Württemberg (Taute 1972).

versely to the shaft (Clark 1958). In addition, blunt-ended arrows of wood were made which, to judge from their resemblance to those used extensively over northern Eurasia and north America and shot from crossbows in Finland as late as the nineteenth century, may well have been used to shoot birds or small furred animals like squirrels without damaging their pelts (Clark 1952a, 37). The almost invariable occurrence of beaver and marten bones from Maglemose sites is a reminder that furs were already playing a significant role in the economy of northern Europe. Other resources made available by hunting were the antlers, bones and teeth of the victims. Analysis of the uses made of the various parts of the skeletons of different animals (Clark 1975, 114–23) by Maglemose man reminds us of the fine discrimination exercised by Mesolithic craftsmen in the choice of raw materials.

FISHING AND COASTAL RESOURCES

The Mesolithic inhabitants of northern Europe drew upon birds, fish, marine mammals, shell-fish and plants for sustenance, as well as land mammals. Several kinds of waterbird are represented in food refuse but none of them in quantities sufficient to suggest that fowling was more than an ancillary resource. The widespread, though never abundant, occurrence of white-tailed or sea eagle (*Haliaetus albicilla*) may perhaps be explained by the esteem in which its pinion feathers are widely held for fletching arrows. The need to improve the flight of arrows was of outstanding importance in a mesolithic context (Clark 1948a, 127–30).

A territory so well provided with lakes and rivers possessed rich freshwater fish resources and some at least of these were systematically exploited by Mesolithic man. The largest fish caught was the sheat fish (*Siluris glanis*), but the only species to contribute substantially to food resources was the pike (*Esox lucius*) (Clark 1948b, 57–60; 1952a, 45–8; 1975, 142f). This was important both on account of its size and because when dried or salted it could be stored and so act as a reserve in time of dearth. It could also be caught without too much difficulty and in a variety of ways. At any season, but especially during the winter, the voracity of the pike made it a ready prey to live-bait secured to a hook, and during the spring it could be taken in basket traps or weels as it sought to penetrate inlets or channels to spawn, or again by means of spears or leisters, all devices documented in the archaeological record. Another was the seine net made by knotting threads made from bast fibre, weighting them with stones and suspending them from bark floats.

There is no way of testing exactly when sea fisheries were established in this part of the world because the earlier post-glacial coastlines were submerged by the sea as it rose eustatic-ally with the final melting of the Pleistocene icesheets. One of the few opportunities we have is in parts of Scandinavia where this was more than matched at certain periods by the speed of isostatic recovery of the land and where in consequence the possibility exists of testing middens on old beaches exposed to view above modern sea-level (Clark 1977a). Exploration of a midden at Bua Västergård, Goteborg, for instance, has shown that a line fishery featuring cod, ling and (later on) haddock had been established by at least 5000 B.C. (figure 15). The bones of cod and haddock from middens on Litorina shorelines show that a similar fishery was flourishing off the coasts of Jutland and Zealand during the fourth millennium B.C. (Clark 1948b, app.11). Again we know from excavations at Morton, Fife, that a fishery for cod and haddock had been established at least by the fifth millennium on the opposite side of the North Sea (Coles 1971, 351ff). It follows that sea-going boats must have been active in the north at least by Late Mesolithic times, a fact of some considerable importance in relation to the early transmission of culture.

A problem yet to be solved is how far the increased evidence for marine food during the later or Atlantic phase of the north-ern Mesolithic is due to the simple accessibility of the data from that time and how far to the pressure exerted on terrestrial resources exerted by the progressive encroachment of the sea during the Flandrian transgression in western Europe and the

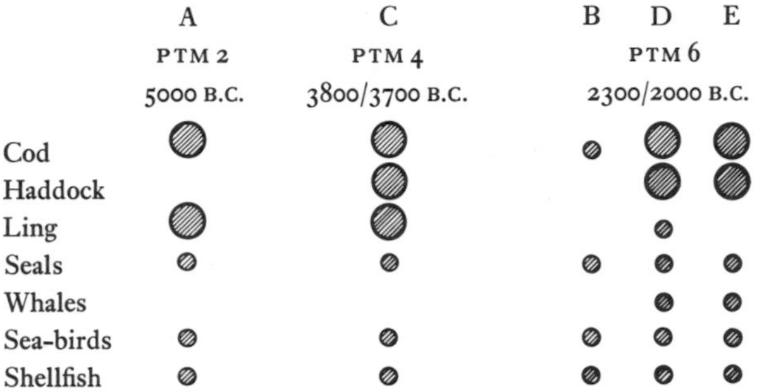

	A	C	B	D	E
	PTM 2	PTM 4		PTM 6	
	5000 B.C.	3800/3700 B.C.		2300/2000 B.C.	
Cod	◉	◉	◌	◉	◉
Haddock		◉		◉	◉
Ling	◉	◉		◌	
Seals	◌	◌	◌	◌	◌
Whales				◌	◌
Sea-birds	◌	◌	◌	◌	◌
Shellfish	◌	◌	◌	◌	◌

Figure 15. Evidence for early marine line fishery off west Sweden.

local Litorina phases in the Baltic. In addition to fish the sea mammals that preyed upon them, such as seals (Clark 1946) and toothed whales (Clark 1947; 1952a, 67), themselves afforded food for man. The most important included grey seals, which were probably culled just before the pups took to the sea, and porpoises, which were still being hunted down to near the end of the nineteenth century by guilds of hunters as they passed through the Little Belt between Fünen and Jutland on their way out of the Baltic. The mounds formed by accumulations of the shells of cardium, mussels, oysters and other marine molluscs on successive Litorina shorelines document the collection and consumption of shell fish, but analysis has shown that this can hardly have provided more than a minor part of the food requirement even of groups within reach of the coast (Clark 1975, 192f). The main value of this resource was that it was available when others might fail.

VEGETATION

The animal refuse incorporated in the Danish shellmounds suggests that they were deposited by men who depended to a large extent, as their predecessors had done, on terrestrial resources. The most pervasive of these was probably vegetation. Here the picture is more than usually distorted by defective collection of the primary data. The tradition of salvaging plant residues, in particular those readily visible on visual inspection, notably charcoals and nuts, is one established long ago in northern archaeology. Yet even there the main motive was palaeobotanical: material was sorted out of archaeological deposits to establish its context in the Postglacial vegetational succession. It is only since Hans Helbaek began to devote himself to the systematic collection and interpretation of plant remains from archaeological sites as a source of information about their economic role in ancient society that a real beginning has been made. So far the evidence is still slight. Such as it is it suggests that by an early stage of the Mesolithic the north Europeans had already started on effective exploration of the food potential of the indigenous flora. Thus, of the nine marsh and open community plants identified from Star Carr, traces of six were found in the intestines of bog corpses from the Roman Iron Age of Denmark and the other three were still being eaten by European peasants down to the nineteenth and twentieth centuries A.D. (Clark 1975, 145 table 9). The probable importance of the plant component of Mesolithic diet was closely examined by Clark (1976).

THE FINAL PHASE

The conditions prevailing during the final phase of the Mesolithic varied. Whereas in the Mediterranean,[4] along the Atlantic seaboard[5] and as far north as the west Baltic region the continuing eustatic recovery of sea-level entailed a progressive loss of land, complicated at the northern end by some minor fluctuations, this was offset in the north Scandinavian area by isostatic recovery and a consequent gain of land. By and large geographical change worked in favour of intensifying the quest for food, among other ways by enhancing the role of fishing and above all by adopting elements of farming economy. Yet the northward spread of farming was at all times

4. A. C. Blanc found that in Lower Versilia, on the east side of upper Italy, sea level was as much as 90 m lower at the peak of the last glaciation. This gives a fair measure of the extent of the Postglacial transgression. See Zeuner (1945, 182ff).
5. The Flandrian transgression of G. Dubois.

constrained by the climatic requirements of the principal food crops. In practice the cereals on which European agriculture almost entirely depended in early times were able to spread relatively easily in Greece, the south Balkans and round the shores of the Mediterranean. By contrast it required time for genetic strains to emerge capable of tolerating the progressively colder climates of the more northerly parts of temperate Europe. This, and the fact that there was plenty of new land to the north capable of colonisation by any population rendered surplus by loss of land at times of marine transgression, meant that a Mesolithic way of life was maintained a thousand years or so longer in south Scandinavia than in neighbouring parts of temperate Europe. Further south, on the other hand, Meso-lithic economies persisted for a shorter time and then primarily on lands least favourable to agriculture.

As I pointed out (Clark 1958) and as Mathyushin (1976, fig.48) has recently perhaps overstressed, a leading innovation in lithic technology, the adoption of cutting arrow-heads (trapezoidal, rhombic and transverse), spread rather rapidly over extensive tracts of continental Europe (see figure 16) during its later Mesolithic phase. Even if we make more allow-ance than I originally did (Clark 1958, 40) for the fact that the trapeze is after all only a double version of one of the most elementary forms of microlith, the obliquely blunted point, its spread remains impressive. Blade and trapeze industries extended from Iraq (Braidwood and Howe 1960, pls 18 and 24) and the Caspian shore (Coon 1951, pl.VIII) to the south Urals (Mathyushin 1976, 190ff), across the plains of south Russia to the Crimea (Formazov 1955, Krainov 1960), the Ukraine (Telegin 1966, figs 1,3), Moldavia (Păunescu 1970, figs 17–19), the Middle Danube (Srejović and Letica 1978, Taf.CXIII, 29–32),[6] the Alps (Wyss 1968, Bandi et al. 1964) and Poland (Kozłowski 1972, 319f and tables XXXVI–XLIII). In northern Europe the new fashion appeared in the Kongemose phase

6. For the microlithic industries with trapezes from Šakvice, Moravia, see Klima (1957) and for Sered, south Slovakia, see Bárta (1957, 5ff).

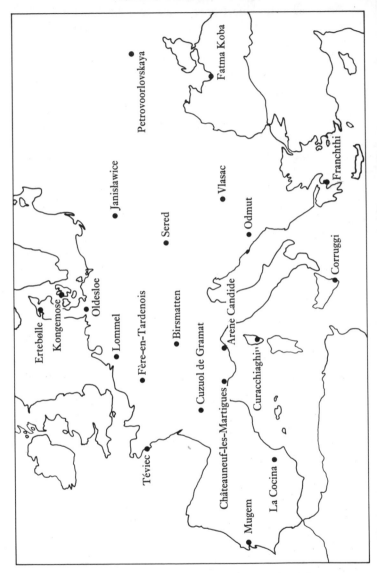

Figure 16. Map of some key Mesolithic sites with blade and trapeze industries in Europe.

(Clark 1975, fig.40)[7] and in western Europe in the Early Tardenoisian and Castelnovian of inland France (Lacam *et al.* 1944, Rozoy 1973).[8]

By contrast the distribution of blade and trapeze industries round the Mediterranean and on the Atlantic seaboard is noticeably discontinuous, suggesting that in this case the diffusion must have been accomplished at least in part by boats. In addition to occurrences on the Mediterranean and Atlantic coasts of France[9] and Iberia,[10] and in Tunisia and east Algeria (Vaufrey 1939), blade and trapeze industries are known from Greece (see p.70), Italy, Sicily (Brea 1949), Sardinia and Corsica (Lanfranchi and Weiss 1973). (For blade and trapeze assemblages with pottery in Italy, see p.90.) In terms of radiocarbon dating, movements overseas have already been documented for the eighth millennium B.C. for the Aegean (see p.70) and the seventh for Corsica.[11] A point on which particular emphasis may be laid is the degree of comparability (figure 17) between blade and trapeze industries in different parts of the Mediterranean from Italy to the south of France, and north Africa, but also in widely separated localities on the Atlantic seaboard, notably the Tagus estuary and the coastal zone of Morbihan. The Mediterranean and Atlantic coastal industries are further linked by a feature that distinguishes them as a group from the classic Tardenoisian of

7. The initial date for the Kongemose phase is K-1526, 5890 ± 140 B.C.
8. According to Rozoy (1978, 329), trapezes first appeared in the sequence at Rouffignac in the Dordogne early in the sixth millennium (GrN-2889, 5850 ± 50 B.C.).
9. For the Mediterranean coast, see de Fonton (1966) and Smith (1952). For the Atlantic see Péquart (1934) and Péquart *et al.* (1937).
10. For the Mediterranean zone, see Pericot (1945). For the Atlantic coast, see Ribiero (1880), Breuil and Zbyszewski (1947) and Roche (1960). A sample from the base of the Moita do Sebastião gave the following date: Sa-16, 5400 ± 350 B.C. The earliest for Cabeço de Armorcira and Arruda were respectively: Sa-195, 5080 ± 350 and Sa-197, 4480 ± 300 B.C.
11. For a determination from a pre-Neolithic level at Curacchiaghiu, see Gif-797, 6610 ± 170 B.C.

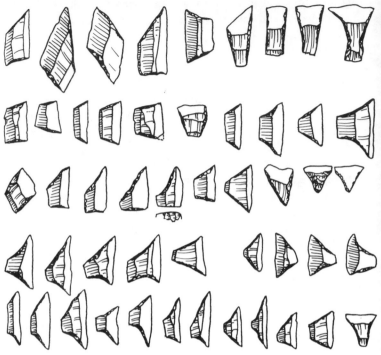

Figure 17. Rhombic and trapeziform microliths from Europe:
(*top row*) Denmark; (*second*) Poland (Janisławice culture) and
Ukraine (4 *right*); (*third*) Inland France (Tardenoisian culture,
early *left*, later *right*); (*fourth*) Châteauneuf-les-Martigues,
Provence, and Corruggi, Sicily (4 *right*); (*bottom*) Cabeço da
Arruda, Mugem, Portugal and La Cocina, E. Spain (5 *right*).

inland France and Belgium, namely the absence of the right-
angled trapeze, the *pointe tardenoisienne typique* of Lacam *et al.*
(1944) and *pointe de Vielle* of Daniel (1948).

THE MESOLITHIC ACHIEVEMENT IN EUROPE

In summary, although the Mesolithic inhabitants of northern
Europe certainly inherited much of their technology and their
general way of life from their Upper Palaeolithic forebears,
they were above all notable for the manner in which they

adapted their economy and technology in the course of Preboreal and Boreal times to the changing ecological conditions
that ensued after the final contraction of the Pleistocene ice-
sheet. Confronted by the forest, they initiated the process of
clearance that in due course opened up the way for farming.
They widened the range of animals and plants of which they
needed to learn the properties for food and industrial use, developed an elaborate seasonal scheduling of resources and even
succeeded in taming wolves and eliciting the domestic dog.
Furthermore, they initiated specialised fisheries at sea as well
as in lakes and rivers. Many of their major advances in technology related to the quest for food. They made a notably greater
use of bows, and tipped and barbed their arrows with microliths. Among fishing gear they invented hooks, basket traps
and nets. They made mattocks with antler heads mounted on
handles, perhaps for grubbing roots or making tread-traps, and
axes and adzes, with flint blades set in antler sleeves perforated
for wooden handles, for working and perhaps for felling timber.

The Mesolithic inhabitants of Europe also took steps to
improve mobility. Although the only direct evidence for
navigation, in the form of the dug-out canoe and the wooden
paddle (Clark 1975, 124), related to inland waters, the indications of marine line fisheries in northern Europe and the overseas movement of obsidian in the Aegean area indicate that
sea-going craft must already have been in use. Again, there is
evidence that the hunter-fisher populations of northern Scandinavia had begun to develop devices for sliding over snow
early in Atlantic times (*ibid.*, 230).

It is also a fact that extensive networks were already developed by hunter-foragers, and this is particularly manifest in
respect of the movement of materials used in lithic industries.
Evidence that this was in full swing well back in the Upper
Palaeolithic in south-west Asia is provided by the occurrence,
although in small quantities, of obsidian from Nemrut Dag,
west of Lake Van, in the Baradostian level at Shanidar some
500 km over the Zagros mountains in a direct line, and from a
yet greater distance in the final Upper Palaeolithic of Zarzi

(Renfrew *et al.* 1966). From Europe it is known that the Magdalenian inhabitants of Gönnersdorf, near Koblenz, obtained a proportion of their flint, up to a fifth in some assemblages, from the chalk of Maastricht, some 120 km distant (Löhr 1975); and again that the makers of the more or less contemporary Swiderian industries of Poland acquired their chocolate-coloured flint from the slopes of the Holy Cross mountains over a radius of up to 200 km (Kozłowski and Sachse-Kozłowska 1975). That exchange networks were still active in Mesolithic Europe is shown, for example, by the occurrence of obsidian from the island of Melos in the Mesolithic level in the cave of Franchthi on the coast of the Peloponnese (Jacobsen 1972) and again, by the use of fine brown quartzite from Wommersom, near Tirlemont, by the makers of microlithic industries over extensive areas of Holland and Belgium as far distant as localities in Flanders 120 km from the source (Clark 1936, 207; for details see Ophoven *et al.* 1948).

It may be assumed as a working hypothesis that long before farming was established in Europe the indigenous population had acquired a working knowledge at least of the raw materials needed to operate their inherited technology. Moreover, as we have just seen, they were already operating networks that had the effect of making these materials more generally available than they were in nature. This is hardly to be wondered at when it is remembered that, in addition to ranging over more or less extensive annual territories in pursuit of seasonal food schedules, hunter-fisher bands must, if only for mere genetic survival, have been incorporated in substantially more extensive social territories (Clark 1972b). The converse is also the case, namely that we need to take account of this when considering the mechanics of cultural diffusion.

4

NEOLITHISATION
OF MEDITERRANEAN AND
TEMPERATE EUROPE

INTRODUCTION

The recent upsurge of interest in the later prehistory of Europe has taken the form, in part, of reacting against the assumption popularised by Childe that the continent was, to begin with, subordinate to south-west Asia in respect of economic development. Childe himself made it clear that his basic theme was the study of European civilisation as 'a peculiar and individual manifestation of the human spirit'. Yet in *The Most Ancient East*, published in 1929, only four years after *The Dawn of European Civilization*, he claimed that European prehistory was 'at first mainly the story of the imitation, or at best adaptation, of Oriental achievements' and on the opening page of *New Light on the Most Ancient East* he went even further, writing that 'one thread is clearly discernible running through the dark and tangled tale of these prehistoric Europeans: the westward spread, adaptation and transformation of the inventions of the Orient'. In so far as Childe was inclined to view Europe as a recipient rather than as a creator of culture, it is hardly surprising that he should have found it difficult to appreciate the early Postglacial inhabitants of Europe at their true worth.

One reason for the reaction against an extreme diffusionist interpretation has been the simple impact of radiocarbon dating. Even on straight uncalibrated dates farming, monuments, including ones of megalithic construction, and metallurgy are now shown to have appeared so much earlier than had previously been assumed that Europe could no longer be seen as hopelessly retarded in cultural development by comparison with south-west Asia. Another has been a deeper appreciation of the unique character of European, as of all other civilisations, together with a more sophisticated understanding of economic change and a fuller knowledge of the process of Neolithisation.

THE PROCESS OF NEOLITHISATION

What processes, then, were involved in the replacement of a Mesolithic by a Neolithic way of life in Mediterranean and temperate Europe? Was it, as the hypothesis of the Neolithic Revolution might suggest, that the new way of life was carried in complete from Asia? Could it, to go to the opposite extreme, have been generated autochthonously among the Mesolithic populations of Europe? Or, was it, as one might prefer to suppose, the outcome of interaction between the indigenous Europeans and exotic influences introduced at least in part by actual newcomers? That such interaction was at any rate possible is suggested by the fact that from a cultural standpoint the Mesolithic inhabitants of Europe and south-west Asia were significantly close. They shared the same Upper Palaeolithic ancestry and, not surprisingly, many of the same attributes. Thus, the aceramic farmers of Palestine, Iran, and Kurdistan, notably at Jarmo,[1] made flint industries with a strong microlithic component, resembling those of most later mesolithic industries in Europe. Again, the flint axes and adzes of the Tahunian of Palestine (Kirkbride 1966, fig.15,4) displayed the same tranchet technique of sharpening as those of the Mesolithic of northern Europe (Clark 1936, figs 32,36,37). Bone artefacts tell a similar story. The barbless fish-hook and the barbed spear-heads of the Natufian, for example (Turville-Petre 1932, 272 and pl.XXVIII), compare closely with those of northern Europe (figure 18; Clark 1975, figs 28 and 25–7). Even the device of fixing flint blades into the slotted handles of

1. As a middle date the excavator and principal investigator favours *c*. 6750 B.C. (Braidwood 1975, 130).

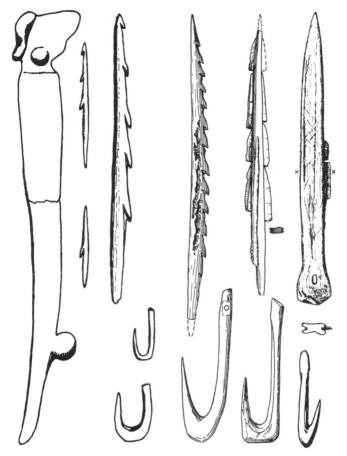

Figure 18. Barbed points, barbless fish-hooks and slotted
equipment from south-west Asia (*left*) and northern Europe.

reaping knives or sickles used by the earliest farmers of south-
west Asia (Solecki 1964, pl.1; Solecki 1963, fig.17; Garrod and
Bate 1937, pl.XIII) had apparently been invented in Upper
Palaeolithic Russia[2] and was widely applied to knives and
projectile heads in Mesolithic assemblages of northern Europe

(see next page for footnote 2)

Figure 19. One of a number of severed heads from
Late Mesolithic (PPN B) Jericho, the face modelled
in plaster and the eyes inset with shells.

(Clark 1975, figs 42–3). Again, the Mesolithic inhabitants of
both Europe and south-west Asia alike made do with containers of non-ceramic materials. More striking still, because
reflecting a common mentality, the practice of burying human
skulls separated from their bodies noted at pre-pottery Jericho
(figure 19) finds parallels in Mesolithic contexts in south
Germany, at Ofnet (figure 20) and Kaufertsberg (Clark 1967,
117–19. See also Schmidt 1912 and Völzing 1935–38, 1ff for
the Ofnet and Kaufertsberg skull finds, and Kenyon 1957 for
the Jericho skulls with plastered faces.).

2. Examples from the Upper Palaeolithic of Russia may be cited
from Taliski, north of Perm in the Urals, and from Kokor'evo,
on the Middle Yenisei. See MacBurney (1976, 27, fig.1 no.9 and
pl.xivb).

Figure 20. Nest of severed heads with attached neck-bones from Ofnet, Bavaria (after Schmidt).

Even in respect of subsistence the gap between hunter-foragers and farmers, not to mention that between 'wild' and 'domesticated' animals and plants, was less sharply defined than most prehistorians were until lately prepared to admit. The stadial heritage of Victorian pseudo-anthropology and the Marxist reconstructions nourished by this combined to blind them to the findings of anthropologists concerned with the systems of food procurement employed by non-industrial societies. The concept of the 'Neolithic Revolution' involved an over-emphasis of the contrast between 'parasitic' and 'productive' modes of subsistence in primitive society. In reality all men, however classified by urban academics, depend on tapping part of the solar energy taken up by plants through photosynthesis. The most direct way of doing this is to harvest plants (whether wild or domesticated), but the same aim can be realised at one or two removes by killing animals (again, whether wild or domesticated) and eating their meat. It is hard to imagine that the change in relationship involved in the 'domestication' of previously 'wild' species, however significant for the development of human society, could have been otherwise than gradual. Instead of considering the communities fossilised in the archaeological record as if the most important thing about them was their ranking in some hypothetical order of progress, we would do better to concentrate on seeking to discover how they in fact obtained their subsistence and why they changed their economic systems or refrained from doing so. The fact that technologically and even ideologically the Mesolithic inhabitants of Europe were at much the same level as their counterparts in south-west Asia, rather than standing either side of a revolutionary divide, allows us to assess the relations between them in more realistic terms, that is more in accord with what really went forward in prehistoric times.

One of the main arguments favouring the hypothesis that the Neolithic way of life, which supplemented and replaced the Mesolithic over extensive parts of Europe during Atlantic times, stemmed wholly from south-west Asia was that the animals and plants on which its underlying economy was based were without exception domesticated there, and must therefore have been introduced to their new habitats. In the case of cultivated cereals this is unquestionably true. Not only were the species cultivated by the earliest farmers in different parts of Europe those first domesticated in south-west Asia, but the wild prototype of only one of them is known from Europe. The exception, einkorn, which occurs in the extreme south-east of Europe in the south Balkans (Nandris 1970, 197), helps if anything to prove the rule. The occurrence in the Balkans is marginal to the main homelands of the wild species, which flourishes best in western Asia Minor and on the hilly flanks of the Fertile Crescent from Palestine to the Zagros (Zohary 1969) where the crucial transformation from foraging to

farming took place in this part of the world. Further confirma-
tion of the essentially exotic origin of the first cereals cultivated
in Europe is the slowness of their expansion (Clark 1965),
reflecting the need of species originally domesticated in a sub-
tropical environment to adapt genetically to successively
cooler zones of climate.

The case is less clear in the case of domestic animals. At least
one species, the dog, had been domesticated by the Mesolithic
natives of northern Europe well before the first crops of wheat
had been harvested even in the Mediterranean zone. It has long
been accepted that Maglemose man possessed the domestic
dog in the west Baltic region by Boreal times, and it has since
been established that the canid skull from Star Carr, dating
back to the middle of the eighth millennium B.C., although
originally identified as wolf, in fact represents a dog (Degerbøl
1961, 53). At the same time revision of the canid remains from
Natufian contexts in Palestine has shown that these relate to
wolf rather than dog (Clutton-Brock 1962). Leaving aside the
status of the canid skull from the Upper Palaeolithic mammoth
hunter station of Mezin in south Russia (Pidoplichko 1969,
fig.33), it is in any case established that the domestic dog
appeared in northern Europe some time before it did in south-
west Asia. The earliest dogs show no sign of the kind of
specialisation one might expect if they had been domesticated
specifically for hunting. On the contrary the way their bones
were intermingled with those of food animals argues that they
were themselves eaten. In this respect they conform to Heere's
concept (1969, 267) that meat was the primary objective of
animal domestication. The essential value of domestic as
opposed to wild animals lies after all in their ready availability.
Because of this dogs would have been of far greater value to
hunting bands in times of dearth than their comparatively
small yield of meat would suggest. They are also valuable in
the present discussion as an indication that the Europeans
were capable of domesticating animals on their own account.

South-west Asia can surely claim priority in the case of
caprines. At Shanidar, for instance, herds of goats were being

managed in a way suggesting that the process of domestication was already under way by the tenth millennium B.C. in the Zagros mountains. Sheep were also taken in hand early in that part of the world and claims for independent taming in western Europe are not well founded. Prototypes are critically absent from Pleistocene deposits in Europe. The few sheep bones from blade and trapeze contexts at Châteauneuf-les-Martigues close to the Mediterranean coast (Ducos 1958), from Tardenoisian levels in the interior of France and from middens on the Breton coast and on the Tagus estuary (Clark 1958, 33) are best explained as the outcome of contact with contemporary farmers. In the case of cattle and swine the position remains ambiguous. Both were hunted by Palaeolithic man in Europe as well as western Asia, and it is arguable that each was domesticated more than once. Forms transitional between domestic cattle and the parent aurochs (*Bos primigenius*) have been claimed as far apart in Europe as Schleswig-Holstein and the Bosphorus (Heere 1969, 265) and a case has been made for Greece despite the fact that conditions have never been outstandingly good there for this species. In respect of the horse the priority of Europe seems incontestable, since the wild species is conspicuously absent from south of the Caucasus. The most likely focus of domestication might seem to have been the steppes of south Russia where the animal had been hunted by Palaeolithic man and was harnessed to wheeled vehicles as early as Neolithic times (Piggott 1968). This helps to show how the economic base of farming was enriched as it spread into territories endowed with resources long exploited, though in a different way, by indigenous populations.

The fact remains that however much it was enriched in Europe the essence of the farming economy was introduced from south-west Asia. Again, although hunting, catching and foraging were capable under the right conditions of providing an adequate as well as a congenial living, it has to be accepted that where ecological circumstances made it practicable even primitive farming was markedly more productive, permitted greater concentrations of population based on more reliable as well as richer sources of food, and therefore favoured a higher degree of social integration, and a more advanced technology. The new economy enjoyed overwhelming competitive advantages over the old. Yet the implications for the indigenous population of the intrusion of farmers or even of elements of farming economy were by no means uniform. There was a clear distinction between the inhabitants of territories best adapted to the new economy, such as the loess lands of central Europe, and those settled in more marginal lands into which farming would only spread when the primary area had been fully exploited at least to the limits of a primitive extensive system. In the territories best adapted to primitive farming the indigenous population had no chance of withstanding the advance of an economy so much more powerful than its own. Again, as is so well documented for the advance of the *Linearbandkeramik* (LBK) over central Europe from Slovakia to northern France and eastwards to Moldavia, extensive farming, based as it probably was on a slash and burn regime, could spread rapidly indeed within the same ecological zone. In such territories the very success of the Mesolithic inhabitants in helping to prepare the way for the spread of the new economy, by initiating inroads on the Postglacial forest and acquiring a detailed knowledge of animals, plants and raw materials, served only to speed their own elimination. In secondary territories, which geographically were so much more extensive, it was very different. Here the degree of cultural comparability, on which I have already insisted, together with their own experience, allowed them to enter into dialogue with their more powerful neighbours and it was precisely through the resulting process of acculturation that they were able to exert a significant influence over the cultural diversity of the greater part of Neolithic Europe. To a prehistorian the degree of diversity both between Neolithic Europe and south-west Asia and between different parts of Europe is in itself enough to dispose of simple diffusion as a sufficient explanation for the transition from Mesolithic to Neolithic in this continent.

GREECE

Since it occupied the part of Europe most accessible from the innovative centres of south-west Asia the land of Greece occupies a key position in relation to the process of Neolithisation. Until recently a main difficulty in the way of useful discussion was the paucity of information about the indigenous population of the country before the appearance of pottery. The situation is now much improved though still calling insistently for research. Already scientific cave excavation in Epirus backed by extended surveys in Thessaly and the Peloponnese has established that the country had been effectively occupied by man at least as far back as the Middle Palaeolithic (Leroi-Gourhan *et al.* 1963, Milojčić *et al.* 1965, Dakaris *et al.* 1967, Higgs 1968). Disappointingly little is yet known of the character and extent of Mesolithic settlement. One of the few well researched sites of this period is the Franchthi cave at the tip of the Argolid (Jacobsen 1969, 1972). The animal material from the Upper Palaeolithic levels (*c.* 10800–8300 B.C.) of the Kastritsa cave in Epirus compares with that from Romanelli in south Italy and is marked by the frequency of equids, the large size of the deer and the sporadic presence of large caprines. In the overlying Mesolithic layers (*c.* 7300–6800 B.C.) red deer was predominant (75–85 per cent) and since the majority of those killed had reached maturity it is presumed to have been hunted. By contrast the economy prevailing during the Neolithic occupation (*c.* 5800–5000 B.C.) differed so markedly that it must have been introduced. Half the sheep, which together with goats and other animals had almost entirely replaced red deer (only 5 per cent), had been killed before maturity, a sign that like cattle, swine and dogs they were already domesticated. Significantly, it was precisely in this context that evidence for agriculture appeared, in the form of remains of emmer, six-row barley and lentils, as well as evidence for the use of pottery.

The one component common to all stages of the Franchthi sequence was the lithic industry. That from the Mesolithic

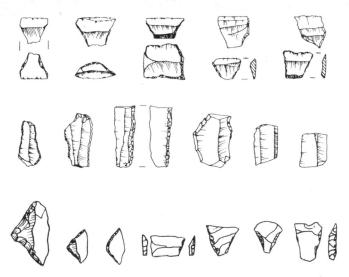

Figure 21. Early lithic assemblages from Greece (approx. 2/3)
(*above*) from PPN level at Argissa, Thessaly (after Theocharis),
and (*below*) from the Mesolithic level at Franchthi cave,
Argolid (after Jacobsen).

level, while carrying forward some traits of the underlying
Upper Palaeolithic, showed two features of outstanding
interest (figure 21, lower). For one thing it included sym
metrical trapezes of the type that had accompanied some of the
earliest farming in parts of south-west Asia and for another
artefacts made from obsidian shown by a conjunction of three
physical tests to have come from a source on the Aegean island
of Melos (Jacobsen 1972, 83ff). The network of interaction
that brought Melian obsidian to Knossos, Crete, during its
initial occupation (stratum x) and in due course as far north
as Nea Nikomedeia in western Macedonia was thus already in
operation by the eighth millennium B.C. (figure 22). Evidence
that boats must have been plying in the east Mediterranean in
Mesolithic times is further suggested by the presence of
microlithic industries on Skyros at present some 35 km east of
Euboea (Weinberg 1965, 8). There are signs that this traffic

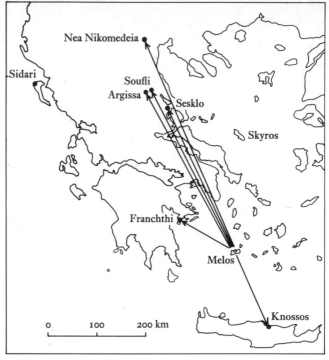

Figure 22. The obsidian network in Greece
prior to the use of pottery.

was linked with the activities of fishermen. The occurrence in
the upper Mesolithic level at Franchthi of fish vertebrae so
large and numerous that they accounted for more than half the
animal bones by bulk from that level recalls the occurrence of
similar bones, in this case identified as tunny, from a late fifth
or early fourth millennium deposit at Saliagos, Antiparos, some
60 km east of Melos (Evans and Renfrew 1968, app.VIII). In
the light of the abundant evidence for overseas traffic during
the Mesolithic phase in the east Mediterranean there is no
problem in visualising the passage of ideas, crops, livestock or
men between the islands and mainland of Greece or by extension between Greece and the Asiatic mainland.

The occurrence of aceramic levels, which nevertheless contained evidence for agriculture in the basal levels of the settlement at Knossos (stratum x) on Crete (Evans 1964, 142; 1968, 267ff) and under three well known mounds in Thessaly, notably Argissa, Sesklo (Milojčić *et al.* 1962) and Soufli (Theocharis 1973, 35), has raised the question whether or not farming reached Greece before potting was introduced and formal Neolithic culture established. The relatively small size of the samples in itself prompts some reserve. Again, even if the absence of sherds is taken at its face value, this need not imply ignorance of potting. It could simply be as Professor Evans (1968, 271) suggested in the case of Knossos that during the initial camping stage the inhabitants were simply not yet organised to engage in potting and made do for a time with containers made from other materials. It remains a striking fact that the only adequate sample of lithic artefacts from aceramic levels under Thessalian tells, that from Argissa (figure 21, upper), has been described by Professor Weinberg (1965, 16) as 'essentially one of blades, often with retouch(e), or of fragments of blades in trapeziform or triangular shape, the well-known microliths', along with awls and scrapers. In Greece, as in south-west Asia, the earliest farmers were linked archaeologically with lithic assemblages of Mesolithic character. As Professor Theocharis (1973, 20–4) was led to comment:

> The chaos which was once thought to exist between the hunting and the food-producing stages is being bridged, and it no longer seems probable that the latter, that is the economy and culture of the Neolithic Period, was transplanted fully developed into a deserted land.

Diffusion there must have been, yet even if detailed analogies can sometimes be drawn between painted wares in Greece and parts of south-west Asia (Holmberg 1964, pl.IV), the fact remains that the Neolithic of Greece like that of every other province of Neolithic Europe was sufficiently idiosyncratic to imply a substantial degree of local development. Although adaptation to differing ecological systems and the insistent need for settled communities to symbolise their separate identities doubtless played a leading part in promoting diversity, the role of indigenous populations should not be overlooked.

SOUTH-EAST AND CENTRAL EUROPE

The distinction between territories colonised initially by cereal farmers and those less immediately suited to the practice of the new economy is nevertheless clearly reflected in lithic industries. Dr Ruth Tringham (1968) was surely right to deplore the comparative neglect of this source. Nevertheless she was able to show quite convincingly that the lithic component of the earliest fully developed Neolithic cultures of Europe, as of south-west Asia, showed a notable absence of the microlithic element found during the formative phase in south-west Asia and even in the initial farming phase of Greece. The story is the same whether one turns to the decorated pottery phase of Greece or those first Temperate Neolithic (FTN) groups, linked thereto by the Vardar-Morava route (Nandris 1970, 205), that flourished in Serbia and west Bulgaria during the later sixth millennium or again to that, defined by *Linearbandkeramik* (LBK), which stemmed from the latter and during the later fifth millennium spread so rapidly over the loess of central Europe from the Vistula to the Rhine. The lithic industries associated with the cereal farmers of south-east and central Europe continued to be based on blades, but these were now supplemented by polished stone axes or adzes. Again they were no longer subdivided to produce trapezes or other forms of microlith. Instead they were adapted to make scrapers, spokeshaves and above all components of reaping equipment (Tringham 1968, fig.10). Although the notion of fitting blades into slotted handles to provide sharp cutting edges for reaping knives was developed long previously during the formative phase in south-west Asia, their role was even more crucial to people who depended so much on harvesting cereal crops as did for example the peasants who made Sesklo pottery in Greece, Starčevo ware further north or LBK ware over extensive tracts of middle Europe. By the same token these peoples had correspondingly less need for hunting equipment and therefore among other things for microlithic armatures. Careful analysis of the animal remains from the extensive site of Bylany in east Moravia for example revealed hardly any wild animals (Clason 1967) in contrast to the wide range of forest species hunted in south-east Europe (Nandris 1978). However, rare traces of Mesolithic traditions are not entirely absent from the archaeological assemblages with LBK ware even within the central area. One could cite for example the short trapeze or transverse arrowhead from an early LBK site at Mohelnice, Moravia (Tichy 1962), or the bone objects decorated with pit ornament from Zauschwitz and Dukovany in the same province (*ibid.*, fig.10 no.1).

The apparent rarity of Mesolithic influence, at least in the lithic component of the more successful LBK farming groups, is all the more striking in view of what has recently been learned about the intensity of early Postglacial occupation of parts of central Europe. Particularly notable are discoveries made in Yugoslavia in the region of the Danubian Iron Gates at sites like Lepinski Vir and Vlasac, and more recently in the cave of Odmut in the former Montenegro (Srejović 1969, 1972, 1977; Srejović and Letica 1978). The organic remains show that the dog was the only domestic animal present between *c*. 8000 and 5500 B.C., when pottery appeared in the context of peasant economy. Catching activities focused on hunting herbivores and fur-bearing animals, supplemented in the case of the Iron Gate sites by fishing. The lithic assemblages found with both groups included microliths of trapeze form, supplemented at the Iron Gates by triangles. Antler and bone were extensively used, among other things, for unilaterally barbed harpoon-heads, scraping tools made from split deer metapodials and, at Lepinski Vir, socketed mattock-heads made from sections of stag antler perforated through the stump of a side tine (figure 23). What makes the pre-ceramic levels at the Iron Gates particularly noteworthy are the architectural traces of several times renewed phases of settlement, each comprising several houses. These were of trapeziform plan with central stone-

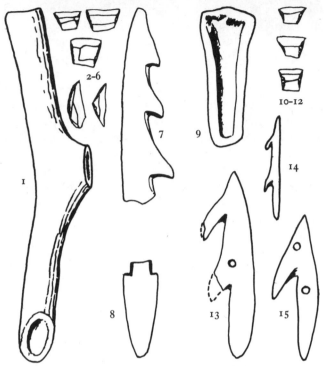

Figure 23. Mesolithic artefacts from Yugoslavia
(*left*) Iron Gate settlements: Lepinski Vir (1) and
Vlasac (2-8); (*right*) the Odmut Cave (9-15).

lined fireplaces, and were apparently covered by ridged roofs
of timbers sloping to the ground in tent-like fashion on either
side (figure 24). The number of graves suggests that in the
aggregate the sites were occupied for a lengthy period. The
eighty-seven graves at Vlasac mainly held extended burials,
sometimes more than one, but there are several indications of
the rite of skull burial known from Palestine and south
Germany. The vigour of the culture is mirrored in the art,
which included decorative geometrical designs applied to antler
and bone artefacts and stone boulders, as well as the more
ambitious fish-face designs pecked on substantial boulders.

74

Figure 24. Reconstruction of Mesolithic house,
Lepinski Vir, Yugoslavia (after Srejović).

Over much the greater part of Europe the situation was very
different. Here we find that hunting, fishing and foraging
frequently played a more significant, if not in some cases a
predominant role in the food quest, and that traces of the
Mesolithic heritage appear not only in flint work, but sometimes in antler and bone work and even occasionally in the
decoration of pottery. It is particularly striking to note this in
territories on the immediate margin of the early zone of Neolithic farming on which attention has already been focused.

Rumania and adjacent parts of the U.S.S.R. provides a useful
test. It is a territory in which the lithic components of Neolithic
assemblages have been notably well studied in conjunction
with those of the local 'Tardenoisian' and it extends from
prime agricultural land to the borders of the steppe. It is
significant that in the case of the LBK settlement of Moldavia,
which incidentally shows a much higher proportion of wild
animal bones than in the case of the Czechoslovak sites, even
Dr Tringham (1968, 65) considered it:

very likely that . . . there was a certain amount of adaptation to different physical conditions, and of contact and
acculturation with the population in the surrounding
areas whose economy was based to a very great extent on
hunting and fishing, and whose blade industry included a
large proportion of geometric microliths.

In the light of Păunescu's (1970) amply documented and
illustrated study of the lithic evidence from Rumania one may
go further and observe that the flintwork of the makers not only
of LBK ware, but also of the earlier Starčevo-Kris and the
partly contemporary Boian wares included the full range of
rhombic and trapezoidal forms of microlith characteristic of
the Rumanian 'Tardenoisian' (figure 25; *ibid.*, figs 18,19). One
can hardly escape the conclusion that extensive acculturation
must have taken place between the indigenous Mesolithic
population and the three Neolithic populations defined in the
archaeological record by their differing pottery and, in the case
of the LBK and Boian, their distinct, if overlapping distribu-
tions (Berciu 1961, pl.1).

The lithic component of the LBK culture has been subject to
exceptionally close scrutiny on the western margin of its zone
of expansion. Both Bohmers and Bruijn (1958/9) and Newell
(1970) have stressed that the industry excavated from settlements in Dutch Limburg is based to a large extent on the
production of blades. These were used to make insets for
reaping equipment, scrapers and burins, but also as blanks for
arrow armatures, including triangular and trapezoidal microliths of a kind used by local Mesolithic populations (figure 26,
upper). A fact brought out particularly well by Salomonsson
(1960) in his study of the flint work from analogous sites at
Belloy-sur-Somme (figure 26, lower) on the loess of northern
France is that the Omalian (LBK) peasants used the same notch
and micro-burin technique for detaching microliths from their
parent blades as the makers of Tardenoisian and even Sauveterrian industries, a fact all the more significant that the
Omalian layer directly overlay a Tardenoisian one. It is hard
to resist the conclusion that at the western as at the eastern

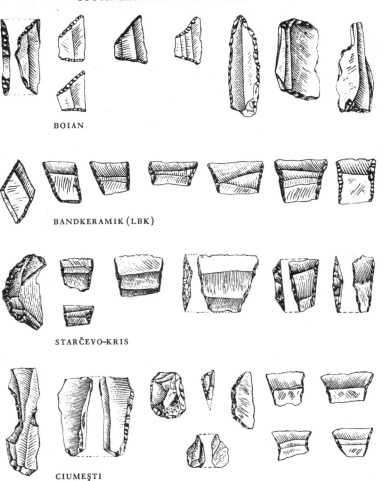

BOIAN

BANDKERAMIK (LBK)

STARČEVO-KRIS

CIUMEŞTI

Figure 25. Blade and trapeze industries (approx. 2/3) from the Mesolithic site of Ciumeşti and from successive phases of the Neolithic in Rumania (after Păunescu).

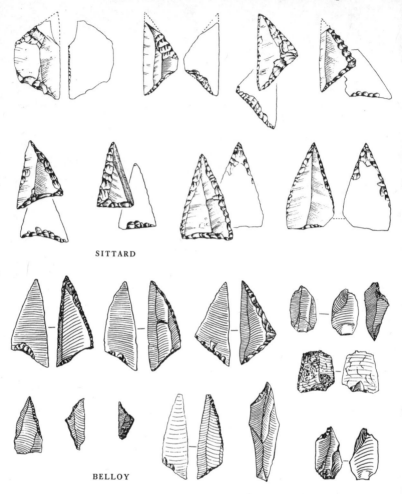

SITTARD

BELLOY

Figure 26. Trapeziform and derivative arrowheads from marginal LBK sites (approx. 2/3): (*above*) Sittard, Limburg (after Modderman), and (*below*) Belloy-sur-Somme, France (after Salomonsson).

extremity of their expansion the makers of LBK pottery underwent acculturation with the local Mesolithic population. The
effect of acculturation appeared on both sides. The Danubians
adopted arrowheads of lop-sided and triangular form, clearly
derived from Mesolithic prototypes but modified among other
ways by the application of a flat-flaking technique. That arrowheads satisfied an economic need on the western frontier of
LBK expansion is shown by the occurrence of triangular,
asymmetric and transverse forms, identical with those from
the Dutch sites and made from Limburg flint, at the late fifth-
millennium Rhenish settlement of Müddersheim (Schietzel
1965). Analysis of the associated fauna showed an unusually
high, though probably exaggerated, proportion of wild
animals.[3] It is worthy of note that the Omalian peasants made
socketed axe-heads of stag antler precisely similar to those in
use about the same time in the Kujavian province of Poland
and during the Ertebølle phase in Denmark, but also to those
made many centuries earlier in a Mesolithic context at Lepinski
Vir.

Both in France and in the Upper Rhenish area indigenous
Mesolithic groups armed with trapezoidal and other microliths
continued to practise their old technology and way of life with
only minor borrowings. Yet, although the makers of Tardenoisian industries in the interior of France continued to hunt
the same animals as their Sauveterrian forebears, rare traces of
domesticated sheep or goat, for example from the Tardenoisian
I level at Cuzoul de Gramat (Lacam *et al.* 1944)[4] and from Le
Martinet, Sauveterre-la-Lémance (Coulanges 1935, 5 and fig.
18), suggest some contact with farmers, as do signs of flat

3. The proportion of animals classified as wild, given as 28.8% by
by the number of bones and 46% by individuals represented, is
almost certainly exaggerated. Doubt arises from the breakdown
of *Bos*, 70% of the total, into 47.8% domestic, 7.2% 'intermediate' and 14.85% aurochs: one has to recognise the possibility that this masks varying degrees of 'domestication'. Other
animals classified as 'wild' include pig (1.35%), horse (1.8%), red
deer (0.9%) and roe deer (0.9%).
4. A single tooth of a domesticated sheep or goat (p.9) came from
levels II-III. These contained a Tardenoisian I industry and
included a triangular arrowhead with flat flaking (fig.12, no.18).

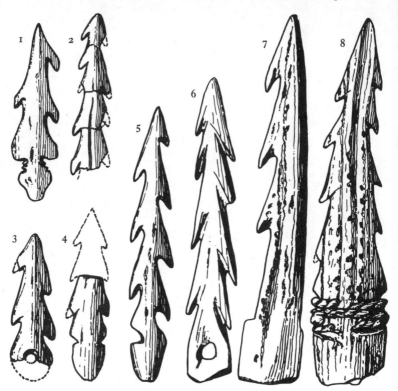

Figure 27. Stag antler harpoon-heads from the Late Mesolithic (1-5) and the Neolithic (6-8) of the Alpine Foreland and south Germany (approx. 1/2): (1) Wachtfelsen, Grellingen, Bern; (2-4) Birsmatten, Bern; (5) Falkensteinhöhle, Tiergarten, Hohenzollern; (6-7) Lattrigen and Bielersee, Bern; (8) Egolzwil 2, Luzern.

flaking on triangular arrow tips from each site. The well-stratified succession at Birsmatten-Basisgrotte (Bandi *et al.* 1964) in the Birstal south of Basel shows that a Tardenoisian industry with trapeziform as well as triangular microliths flourished as late as the latter half of the fourth millennium in radiocarbon terms. A late date has been confirmed archaeologically by the contexts in which antler harpoon-heads (figure

27) like those represented in the Tardenoisian levels at the Basisgrotte occur in near-by parts of South Germany, notably with antler hafts and a polished stone celt in the Falkenstein-höhle near Tiergarten, Hohenzollern (Peters 1934) and with sherds of late LBK sherds in a rubbish pit at Gniessen, Wald-shut on the Upper Rhine (Gersbach 1956). If the local date of these harpoon-heads is late, their similarity to those from the Iron Gate points to a Mesolithic source. Although these finds suggest cultural contact between hunter-foragers and farmers, analysis of the animal bones from Birsmatten shows that meat was derived mainly from pig and red deer and that domestic animals were entirely absent. (The only exception, a single cow bone from stratum 1, was shown from its condition to be a late admixture. Bandi *et al.* 1964, 95.)

THE ALPINE FORELAND

As previously hinted in respect of the West Baltic region, in territories well stocked with game animals and fish an in-digenous population would be able to secure an adequate living without having to submit to domestication. In such an environ-ment an economy based on hunting, fishing and gathering was well founded. Even so it had to give way when its territory was required by farmers during their phase of secondary expansion after initially preferred soils had been taken up. Yet, as Higham's analysis of the data from key Neolithic settlements in the Alpine Foreland has shown, the process was likely to be far more gradual than in a territory better suited to agriculture. That the earlier Neolithic inhabitants in fact continued to rely substantially on wild animals (aurochs, elk, red and roe deer, pig) for their meat is shown in table 4, abstracted from Higham (1968, table 23).

The Mesolithic tradition is much less conspicuous in the artefact assemblages from the early Neolithic of the Alpine Foreland than the economic base might have led one to expect. The microlithic component of the lithic industry is limited to the occasional occurrence of trapeziform microliths like the narrow trapeze from Seematte (von Gonzenbach 1949, taf.7

Table 4. Percentages of wild animals represented at
settlements of different periods in the Alpine Foreland.

Egolzwil 3 (*c.* 3000 B.C.): Older Cortaillod	40%
Seeberg Burgäschisee (mid-third): Younger Cortaillod	42%
Zürich Utoquai (*c.* 2000 B.C.): Corded ware	20%
Zürich Alpenquai (*c.* 750 B.C.): Late Bronze Age	10%

no.22) or the chisel-ended arrowhead. The rather slight information available so far about the non-lithic dimensions of
the Swiss Mesolithic makes it difficult to be explicit about
artefacts in other materials. One might, however, compare the
perforated antler mattock heads and barbed antler harpoon
heads recovered from Neolithic sites with similar objects from
the Mesolithic assemblage from Schotz (Wyss 1968). Again,
the pit ornament on pendants from Cortaillod sites (von
Gonzenbach 1949, taf.11 no.12 and taf.12 nos 4 and 11) would
certainly suggest Maglemose ancestry if found in northern
Europe. Another feature of Swiss Neolithic technology that
points to a Mesolithic origin is the sophisticated use of birch
bark (*ibid.*, taf.5, taf.12 no.13 and taf.13 nos 1–4) for making
small containers, adapted for ornamenting pottery or as a
source of the birch pitch (*birkenteer*) used to haft projectile
heads or the blades of knives and sickles, or even for securing
cut-out patterns of birch bark on pottery bowls.

NORTHERN EUROPE

The Late Mesolithic inhabitants of the north European plain,
including the west Baltic zone discussed in chapter 3, continued to practice their hunter, fisher, forager way of life for
another thousand years or so after their neighbours to the
south had established a flourishing farming economy on the
loess. There is no sign that the Ertebølle inhabitants of
Denmark modified their pattern of subsistence to the slightest
extent (Clark 1975, 196) as a result of any contact through the
intermediate zone of Schleswig-Holstein and adjacent parts of
north Germany with settled farming economies to the south.

The situation is not much different in respect of technology. One of the few features most probably inspired from central Europe was the perforated stone *breitkeil* (*ibid.*, 187 and fig.52) sparsely but widely distributed over Schleswig-Holstein, Denmark and Scania. The coil-built pointed-base Ertebølle pottery (*ibid.*, 184ff), whatever its origin, is an important reminder, paralleled by the oviform impressed wares of Finland (*ibid.*, 229) and large parts of the Soviet Union (Sulimirski 1970),[5] not to mention occurrences as far afield as Japan (Kidder and Esaka 1968) or for that matter North America (Clark 1975), that the ability to make pottery containers was capable of spreading far beyond the range of farming.

Agriculture was first introduced to Denmark from the south about the same time it spread to the Alpine Foreland. The funnel-neck beaker (FNB) ware that came with it had developed on the north European plain between the Weser and the Weichsel as an independent tradition, presumptively as an outcome of acculturation between bearers of Danubian culture and the indigenous Mesolithic population. One way in which the vitality of the latter population manifested itself in Denmark lay in the persistence of significant elements of Ertebølle technology. This is particularly well seen in respect of flint work, for example in the flake axes, end of blade scrapers and short trapezes or chisel-ended arrowheads found not merely in Early Neolithic A contexts at Muldbjerg and Store Valby (Troels-Smith 1935; Becker 1954, figs 17,22,32), but also at the EN C settlement at Havnelev (Mathiassen 1940) and even at the MN III site of Bundsø (Mathiassen 1939, fig.9). The pertinacity of the old technology can also be appreciated by reflecting that it overlapped the introduction, in the thin-butted polished flint axe with flattened sides (Glob 1952, 86f) and the knobbed polygonal polished stone battle-axe (*ibid.*, 85), of key types inspired by leading metal forms of the Danubian III copper age. Although the new economy adopted in the west Baltic area was largely based on imported crops and

5. Pp.90 (E. Baltic), 93-8 (Volga-Oka), 102-7 (Kama-Ural).

livestock, it entered territories settled for seven millennia or so by populations already in command of many resources of food and raw materials, having a technology well adapted to local conditions, including also the ability to navigate at sea, and which had already initiated the process of forest clearance that made possible the expansion of farming.

The aspect of northern Europe during the Later Stone Age most directly relevant to the topic of this essay is that the region straddled the economic divide between territories in which farming provided the basic source of subsistence and those in which hunting, catching and foraging continued to be the most effective ways of securing a living. Taken as a whole northern Europe illustrates on spatial terms what has already been demonstrated stratigraphically in both the Old and the New Worlds, namely the gradual nature of the transition between the two basic modes of subsistence. Although speaking broadly farming was the mode of economy best adapted to the temperate climate and biotypes of south Scandinavia and different forms of catching and foraging to the ecology of Fennoscandia proper, the division was by no means sharply drawn. Even in the farming zone catching activities might predominate locally as they appear to have done on the coast of Bohuslän. The picture was even more complex in the north.[6] There was not merely a wide range of choice and emphasis in respect of catching activities, but locally livestock and even cereal crops might contribute, even if in a subsidiary manner, to the economy. Beyond question the subsistence economies of Fennoscandian communities were notably more various than those existing in the farming zone and surely need to be studied on a local basis.

6. This is a topic I hope to treat in *The Later Stone Age Settlement of Scandinavia*. One of the best available sources is still chapters VI and VII of Schetelig and Falk (1937). For the taiga zone of north-west Russia, the section on 'The culture of the hunters and fishers of north-eastern Europe' in Gimbutas (1956, 177-213) may be consulted.

THE MEDITERRANEAN BASIN

If the Balkan peninsula and the south Russian plains provided effective routes for the spread of farming into temperate Europe overland, the Mediterranean offered direct access to the evergreen zone of southern Europe, which for ecological reasons was more accessible to an economy first developed in south-west Asia. To anyone capable of navigating it the sea offered relative ease of movement at a time when transport over land was at best rudimentary. The discovery of large fish bones, which are most likely to have been tunny, in the Mesolithic level in the Franchthi cave at the very time that Melian obsidian appeared in the sequence suggests that the tunny fishery, surely documented for the fifth at Saliagos, may well also have been practised in the eighth millennium. Once established in any region tunny fisheries were inherently liable to spread since, once a coastline frequented by tunny shoals was filled with its complement of trap weirs (Fodera 1961), there was no way of increasing the catch other than by exploring and developing additional grounds. Tunny fishers had a strong motive for exploring new coasts and in this they must often have been aided by the movements of tunny shoals themselves. This makes it all the more suggestive that the discontinuous distribution of blade and trapeze industries and no less of shell-impressed ware pottery in the Mediterranean basin coincides substantially with that of the most productive tunny fisheries of antiquity (Höppener 1931, 180).[7] At the very least it is likely that fishermen played a key role in opening up a knowledge of the geography of the Mediterranean basin to the relatively advanced peoples of Greece and its neighbours. In making new fishing grounds available it goes without saying that pioneers would have opened up new possibilities to land-based farmers.

Radiocarbon determinations from a pre-ceramic deposit at Curacchiaghiu, Lévie, South Corsica (Lanfranchi and Weiss

7. I am indebted to Professor J. A. Crook of St John's College, Cambridge, for this reference.

1973)[8] suggest that fishermen-navigators had already reached the west Mediterranean by the mid-seventh millennium B.C. In this case they can hardly have been any other than Mesolithic. This makes it the more unfortunate that the few scraps of lithic material from the level were insufficient for cultural diagnosis. The earliest occurrence of a blade and trapeze industry from the west Mediterranean appears so far to be that represented by the Castelnovian assemblages from the pre-ceramic level at the site of Châteauneuf-les-Martigues in Provence (de Fonton 1966). Although this assemblage, counterpart of the Tardenoisian I of inland France, was not directly dated at this particular site, it appeared at Rouffignac around 5850 B.C. and at Châteauneuf itself was overlaid by a deposit with the same lithic tradition accompanied by impressed ware with a radiocarbon date in the mid-sixth millennium.[9] It is unfortunate that this cannot be checked further east on the north Mediterranean coast at Arene Candide, where there is a gap of some four millennia in radiocarbon terms between the impressed ware levels and the immediately underlying one with an early Mesolithic industry of epi-Gravettian (or epi-Romanellian) tradition (Brea 1946, 1956).[10]

Italy may yet prove to have experienced the impact of late Mesolithic hunter-foragers equipped with a blade and trapeze lithic industry. The stratigraphy of the cave of Corruggi, Pachino, in south-east Sicily is suggestive. Although not as closely documented as a more recent excavation would have been, it is significant that the excavator noted that impressed and incised sherds were restricted to the upper half of the blade and trapeze deposit (Brea 1949). Again, the fact that

8. I owe this reference to Mr J. G. Lewthwait. The radiocarbon determinations are: Gif-797, 6610± 170 B.C. and Gif-1963, 6350± 130 B.C.
9. A radiocarbon date for the early impressed ware level has been determined as KN 5570± 240 B.C.
10. The Early Mesolithic level is dated to (R-100) 8380± 95 B.C., and impressed ware levels 25 and 25/6 to (Pi-27b) 4537± 175 and (R-101) 4270± 55 B.C.

basically the same blade and trapeze component was common not merely to the early Neolithic with impressed ware but also to middle and some late Neolithic assemblages in Italy suggests that it relates either to the population indigenous to Italy at a time when a Neolithic way of life first began to infiltrate to Italy or that it formed part of the impressed ware culture itself.

Since Bernabò Brea (1950) first recognised the importance of pottery decorated by cardium impressions in the Mediterranean, radiocarbon dating has confirmed it as the earliest ceramic to appear in the central and western parts of the basin, with dates ranging from the fifth to the sixth millennium B.C. (Guilaine 1979). One result of the fame of cardial impressed ware has been to attract to itself wares whose only factor in common has been the employment of means for roughening the surface in a decorative fashion. These included pottery ornamented by pinching the surface, such as that from the south Balkan Starčevo culture (Milojčić 1949, taf.29 nos 1–2; Garašanin 1958) which penetrated Greece as far as Thessaly during the final phase of its Early Neolithic (Rodden 1962, 267ff; cf. Holmberg 1964, 10). It is even a fact that impressions of finely toothed combs (Holmberg 1964, cf. Weinberg 1965, 29) from this same horizon have at times been mistaken for imprints of cardium shells. If as the best authorities agree (Brown 1965) we concentrate on true cardial ware, in which by the way the shell edge was quite often applied by a rocker motion, the distribution is found to concentrate on the central and west Mediterranean. A possible source of inspiration has long been sought for this in shell-impressed wares from pre-Halafian levels at sites like Mersin and Ras Shamra on the east Mediterranean coast, as well as further inland, as at Hama and Tell Judeidh or even Chagar Bazar, Arpachiyah and Nineveh. However that may be the discontinuous distribution of cardial ware on the coasts and islands of the central and western Mediterranean must surely point, as Bernabò Brea recognised, to a maritime spread (figure 28). This affected either shore of the Adriatic, on the west from Apulia to Marche (Lollini 1965) and on the east from Corfu and the Ionian islands to the Yugo-

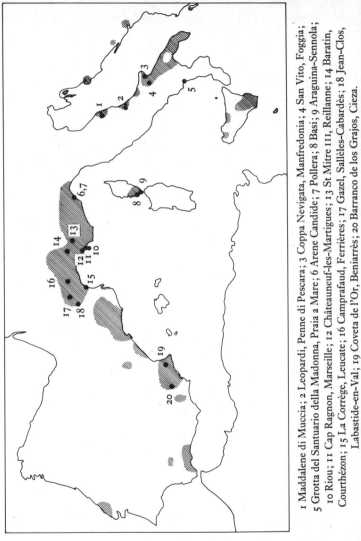

1 Maddalene di Muccia; 2 Leopardi, Penne di Pescara; 3 Coppa Nevigata, Manfredonia; 4 San Vito, Foggia; 5 Grotta del Santuario della Madonna, Praia a Mare; 6 Arene Candide; 7 Pollera; 8 Basi; 9 Araguina-Sennola; 10 Riou; 11 Cap Ragnon, Marseille; 12 Châteauneuf-les-Martigues; 13 St Mitre III, Reillanne; 14 Baratin, Courthézon; 15 La Corrège, Leucate; 16 Camprafaud, Ferrières; 17 Gazel, Sallèles-Cabardès; 18 Jean-Clos, Labastide-en-Val; 19 Coveta de l'Or, Beniarrès; 20 Barranco de los Grajos, Cieza.

Figure 28. Map of cardial impressed pottery in central and west Mediterranean. Numbers indicate sites dated to the sixth and early fifth millennia B.C.; (1–5) impressed (undifferentiated), and (6–20) cardial impressed.

slav islands of Cres and Krk (Alexander 1972, 38); Malta, Sicily, the Lipari Islands, Sardinia and Corsica; the Ligurian coast of northern Italy and the coasts of southern France, Catalonia and Valencia (Aparisi 1950); and, not least in interest, it passed through the straits of Gibraltar to the region of the Tagus estuary (Leisner 1966).

It is commonly held that the onset of Neothermal conditions brought a marked shift both in Italy and in neighbouring territories from reliance on big game to a growing emphasis on coastal resources (Whitehouse 1968, 354ff; 1969). This in turn would have encouraged a more sedentary mode of life and consequently made the indigenous population more receptive to pottery and, within the limits of local environments, to the practice of farming. No one familiar with Mediterranean strands could possibly be surprised at the use of *Cardium* shells for ornamenting pottery. Although commonly occupying the same caves and rock-shelters as their mesolithic predecessors, as at Châteauneuf-les-Martigues, in an extensive territory like Apulia the makers of impressed ware have left behind them enclosures, round houses and storage-pits, the common traces of early European peasant communities. Again, it should not be forgotten that it was makers of such pottery who initiated the settlement that gave rise without apparent break to the temple structures and tombs of Malta (Evans 1959).

The degree of continuity noted by Ruth Whitehouse in the Italian Neolithic is reflected in the persistence of blades and trapezes (figure 29). This is well seen in the vertical sequence at Arene Candide. Microlithic trapezes occurred in the Early Neolithic level with cardial impressed pottery as they did in the Vhò, Fiorana and Gaban Early Neolithic groups of north Italy (Bagolini and Biagi 1977). They persisted in the square-mouthed Middle Neolithic levels at Arene Candide as they did in the Ottara Valley near Cittaducale, Latium (Acanfora 1962–1963), in the former case together with triangles and crescents. Chisel-ended arrowheads continued in use during the Lagozza or Late Neolithic phase in north Italy, though in this case admittedly in derivative form, the sides with flat trimming

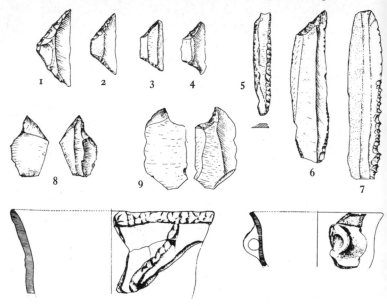

Figure 29. Blade and trapeze component of Middle Neolithic level F in the Ottara Valley, Cittaducale, Italy (after Acanfora). (Sherds approx. 1/6; 1, 5, 8, 9 approx. 5/4; 2, 3, 4, 6, 7 approx. 5/8).

rather than steep lateral retouch (Bagolini and Biagi 1977, fig.9).

Blades and trapezes, sometimes with other forms of microlith, were also an integral part of Neolithic assemblages in the south of France, east and south Spain and south Portugal. This applied not merely to impressed ware assemblages,[11] but also for example to Chassey ones in the south of France (Bailloud and de Boofzheim 1955, pl.XLIII), as it did to Lagozza ones in Italy (*ibid.*, pl.XLII). Furthermore, as the Leisners (1943, 1951; Leisner 1966) have brought out so clearly, blades and trapezes were linked with a wide range of Iberian megalithic

11. For example at Châteauneuf-les-Martigues, Provence (de Fonton 1966, figs.5, 6 and 9) or the cave of Sarsa, Bocairente, Valencia (Aparisi 1950, figs.4 and 5,10,12).

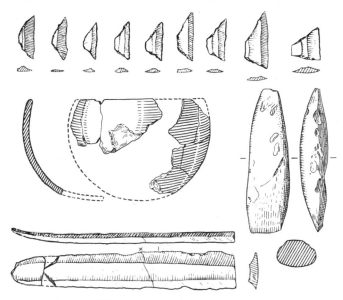

Figure 30. Flint and stone artefacts from Passage Grave 1
at Poço da Gateira, Monsaraz, Portugal (after Leisner).

tombs including passage-graves (figure 30), gallery-graves
and cists as well as open settlements like El Garcel[12] and La
Gerundia (Bailloud and de Boofzheim 1955, 80) in Almeria, in
the latter case with bifacially flaked arrowheads, idols and other
'chalcolithic' traits. In the case of Portugal V. Leisner even
went so far as to claim the link between megaliths and microliths as evidence for the indigenous origin of the tombs.[13]

12. The Leisners followed Siret in arranging Iberian assemblages
in time on typological grounds assuming degrees of poverty to
represent relative antiquity. In this they were still being followed
by Savory (1968, 79). The view more widely shared today is that
El Garcel was relatively late in the sequence; see Arribas (1966,
14).
13. Thus V. Leisner (1966, 369): 'Die Megalithkultur bewahrt
durch ihre ganze Lebensdauer die Bindung an die Mikrolitik: ein
Bewis ihres einheimischen Ursprungs'.

THE ATLANTIC SEABOARD

I began this study by identifying the dichotomy between the predecessors and the heirs of the so-called 'Neolithic Revolution' as a stumbling-block to the understanding of prehistory. Let us see the effect of breaking down this division in seeking to resolve one of the main puzzles of European archaeology, the genesis of the megalithic chamber tombs and associated circular and linear monuments of earth, stone and timber of the Atlantic zone. We are so accustomed to regarding these as the most incontrovertible as well as the most prominent symbols of a specifically Neolithic way of life that you may think me perverse. Yet when a lock has proved resistant for so long one ought to hesitate before condemning any key as inappropriate. And, of course, the key I propose to insert could only be thought inappropriate on the very assumption that I have sought to undermine.

Since the more elaborate megalithic and related rock-cut tombs were designed to receive burials from social groups over periods of time, serving in effect as monumentally contrived cemeteries for particular groups, it may be useful to begin by considering the background to this rite. First, the custom of using inhabited caves as cemeteries is as old as ceremonial burial itself. From Middle Palaeolithic times one may cite the ten Neanderthaloid burials in the Mugharet es-Skhūl, Mount Carmel (Garrod and Bate 1937, 97–107). A larger and more fully documented cave cemetery is that dating from the Early Natufian occupation of the Mugharet el-Wad (*ibid.*, 14–19) in the same locality, comprising some fifty-nine burials. It is particularly worthy of note that this cave provides evidence for collective burial, not indeed in the sense that successive burials of a particular social group were placed in the same chamber, for none such existed. It was merely that members of the same group were interred over a period in the same place of burial, which also happened to be the place of habitation. The ten individuals in chamber 1 were buried in three layers and the much larger number on the platform included groups of five and seven successive interments.

An alternative mode of disposing of the dead practised by the Mesolithic population of the Atlantic seaboard of western Europe was to use parts of their shell-mounds as cemeteries. Some 120 burials were recovered during the early excavations in the Arruda and Moita do Sebastião middens at Mugem on the Tagus estuary (Ribiero 1880) and another 34 were uncovered during later excavations at the latter (Roche 1960, ch. VI). Although the cemeteries in the midden deposits at Hoëdic (Péquart 1934) and Téviec in Morbihan on the south Breton coast were smaller, numbering 13 and 23 inhumations, they have yielded fuller information. In particular those at Téviec (Péquart et al. 1937, ch.III) provide evidence for successive burials, one (II) comprising three and another (K) six individuals. A more specialised form of collective burial is implied by nests of skulls found in caves and rock-shelters in south Germany, notably at Ofnet and Kaufertsberg near Nördlingen (Schmidt 1912) and at Hohlestein, Lonetal, near Ulm (Völzing 1935–8). Signs of cutting on the upper neck vertebrae suggest that the skulls had been detached from their trunks shortly after death. Their numbers, one nest at Ofnet comprising twenty-seven and another six skulls (figure 19), suggest that they relate to social groups comprising in all probability a number of hunting bands. Again their condition, those in the middle showing signs of having been pushed together and those on the periphery relatively intact and undisturbed, argues that, as in the later chamber tombs, they had been buried over a period of time. These skull burials are doubly relevant to my theme. They emphasise the spiritual affinity between the Mesolithic inhabitants of south Germany and the so-called 'PPN' people of the Levant, who practised the same rite with the added elaboration in the latter case of representing the faces of the deceased in plaster. Moreover they exemplify in however specialised a form the rite of collective burial practised by the makers of impressed pottery in many parts of the middle and west Mediterranean (Evans 1958,

51–8), not to mention the builders of artificial tombs whether cut from the living rock or built from megalithic blocks or by dry-stone walling. It may thus be taken as established that the Mesolithic peoples both of Europe and the Levant commonly buried their dead in cemeteries on living sites over periods of time whether in caves, rock-shelters or open settlements and their associated middens.

The next question to ask is whether or not they constructed or were capable of constructing funerary monuments. One certain fact is that the construction of ritual monuments including those associated with death was not a monopoly of societies based on food-production. To take only a single instance from ethnography, the technology of the Australian aborigines, while adequate for their needs, was elementary by comparison with that prevailing almost everywhere else in the world, and there is no question but that they gained their living entirely by hunting, catching and foraging. Yet, as is well known (Clark 1977b, 480–2 and figs.286–7) they were not only capable of building ritual mounds over the dead (figure 31), but constructed alignments of orthostatic stones and made bora grounds approached in some cases by avenues primarily in connection with initiation ceremonies. Although they shifted lesser volumes of earth and erected smaller stones than was often the case in Neolithic Europe, it can hardly be denied that they conceived of analogous structures, however different in scale.

Since archaeological is preferable to ethnographic evidence in interpreting the past I would only point to a monumental burial structure erected about 7,000 years ago in Labrador by men entirely dependent on hunting, catching and foraging. I refer to a burial cairn excavated in 1974 at l'Anse Amour, Strait of Belle Isle (McGhee and Tuck 1975, 85–92). The cairn, consisting of a metre-thick heap of stone boulders some eight metres in diameter, overlay a coffer-like construction, possibly a ritual hearth because containing traces of burning. Directly below this feature the excavators found the extended burial of a man accompanied by a wide range of objects made

Figure 31. Aboriginal burial mound and earthwork, Lachlan River, N.S.W., 1817. Note symbolic carvings on trees.

from bone, ivory and stone. A feature of the Mesolithic midden cemetery of Téviec[14] was that each of the multiple burials (H and K) was surmounted by a ritual stone-built hearth. It is at least suggestive that similar features, some accompanied by traces of burning, were incorporated in Neolithic burial structures in the same district. For example the Manio I long mound (Péquart *et al.* 1937), which was itself overlaid by the stone alignments of Kermario, covered a number of these coffers (Piggott 1937; cf. Bailloud and de Boofzheim 1955, 112ff and pl.xlviii). Although this might suggest that the Mesolithic inhabitants of Morbihan may have contributed directly to the genesis of a type of local Neolithic funerary structure, another feature of this same monument, the wedge-shaped peristalith of small stones that enclosed most of the stone coffers or fire-places under the Manio I mound, recalls the trapezoidal funerary structures of Kujavia built by the makers of funnel-neck beakers in Poland (Chmielewski 1952, 106), a type of monument which also sometimes incorporated ritual stone fire-places. Other analogues include domestic house structures associated with the immediately preceding Lengyel culture of north-central Europe (Jazdzewski 1938) and more relevantly the much earlier trapezoidal house structures of the Iron Gates (figure 24).

This is not the moment to embark on a considered discussion of the origins and development of the diverse forms of megalithic structure or even of chamber tombs in Europe. I would only like to touch on the distribution of such monuments in the light of Dr Kaelas' treatment (1966) of the problem posed by the chamber tombs of south Scandinavia at the ultimate extreme of a distribution extending round the continental shelf of western Europe and into the west Mediterranean basin. Although the recent excavations at Vedbaek not far north of Copenhagen have since shown that the Danes were already burying their dead in cemeteries by *c.* 4000 B.C., 22 graves being found in the undisturbed part of the Bøgebakken site

14. For a useful account of Natufian burial practices, see Anati (1963). For details on 'Einan see Perrot (1957, 1960, 1966).

(Albrethsen and Petersen 1976), there is no evidence from this area for successive burials in the same grave nor has any trace of monumental structure of Mesolithic age been noted in Scandinavia. Nothing discovered since she wrote contradicts Dr Kaelas' assumption that the megalithic idea can hardly have been of autochthonous growth in south Scandinavia and must therefore have arrived from elsewhere. It must either have spread as an idea or been introduced by actual immigrants. Dr Kaelas was fully aware of the objection against the idea of immigration that the contents of chamber tombs in different parts of Europe reflect rather faithfully the cultures prevailing in the several regions. What nevertheless inclined her to accept this alternative was the appearance in south Scandinavia of highly specialised exotic features such as the passage-graves with lateral chambers clustered in the Limfjord region of northern Jutland or the recurrence of twin passage-graves in Denmark and Brittany, neither of which one might have thought precludes the alternative hypothesis. However, that may be, the point I wish to stress here is that in either case, to quote Dr Kaelas, 'the culture contacts or displacements of people involved must in all instances have been maritime'. Particularly revealing in this connection is Dr Kaelas' considered view incorporated in her well-known distribution map (figure 32; Kaelas 1966, pl.11) that the orthostatic passage-graves resembling most closely those of south Scandinavia are to be found in widely separated groups on the Atlantic and west Mediterranean seaboards, namely in Almeria, north-west Iberia, Brittany and north-west Ireland.

The history of geographical discovery records a diversity of motivation. Separately or more often in combination rare materials, land, potential converts, slaves or subjects and not least, as I shall suggest, fish have all helped to lure men to explore beyond the bounds of their own familiar territories. The special attraction of the sea as against the need to break through defended land frontiers is obvious enough, its unfamiliarity and the technical difficulties of navigation among its no less evident drawbacks. If we except crossing open water

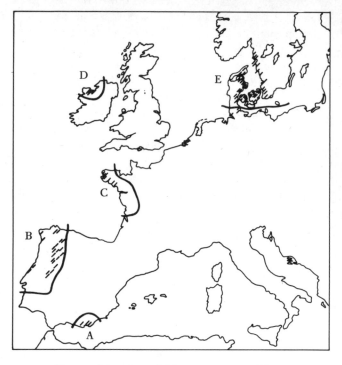

Figure 32. Map of megalithic passage-graves of Europe, defining groups most comparable with those of south Scandinavia (after Kaelas).

to visible land-falls, the pursuit of fish must surely have been among the first things to lead men to build boats and navigate at sea (Bowen 1972, 113). The quest for cod played an important part in opening up the coasts of Newfoundland to Europeans during the late sixteenth and the seventeenth centuries. There are signs that quests for the same fish may have helped significantly in opening up the sea routes implied by the megalithic tombs of the Atlantic seaboard. In a recent essay (Clark 1977a) I argued that the notable group of *dysse* and passage-graves strung out along the coast of Bohuslän, west Sweden, were built by communities who lived substantially by catching cod, haddock and ling, bottom feeders taken on hook and lines from boats either in the Skagerrak or beyond or during the spawning season closer inshore. Certainly there is plenty of evidence for contacts across the water between different parts of south Scandinavia at a time when passage-graves were being built. Such are reflected for example in detailed analogies both in tomb construction and in ceramic decoration between Bohuslän and north Jutland and again between Scania and Zealand (Kaelas 1953; Strömberg 1971, 199). The point to be emphasised in the present context is that the line fishery from the Bohuslän coast was established by the local mesolithic population certainly by *c*. 5000 B.C. (Wigforss 1971; Lepiksaar 1971) in radiocarbon terms (figure 15), that is two-and-a-half millennia before passage-graves began to be built in that part of the world. There is no reason for regarding this as exceptional. We have seen how early sea fishing was established in the Mediterranean. Nearer home Dr J. M. Coles (1971, 351ff) has shown that the Mesolithic fishermen of the Fife coast were already landing large cod, probably over a metre long in some cases, at least as early as the fifth millennium B.C.

In discussing the economic basis of the concentration of v-shaped or Entrance Graves on the Scilly Islands, I recently emphasised that these tombs were far too numerous to account for solely in terms of farming (Clark 1977a, 43). The obvious alternative was to suggest that fishing was a key source of wealth, a suggestion reinforced by the occurrence of this type of tomb in Morbihan and on the margins of the Celtic Sea in west Cornwall and on the coast of Wexford. From this I went on to suggest that fishermen may well have extended their range of geographical knowledge involuntarily by following the seasonal movements of shoals. It is significant that the range of the hake (gen. *Merluccius*), known to have been a key fish in the Celtic Sea during historical times (Went 1952) from the West Mediterranean to the Atlantic seaboard of Iberia, Brittany and north-west Ireland to south-west Scotland, included each of the four areas of passage-grave distinguished by Dr Kaelas as related most closely to south Scandinavia.

During the historical period the hake fishery of the Celtic Sea is known to have attracted fishermen from France and even Biscayan Spain. Further it is significant that hake come into shoal water, where they can most readily be caught with simple tackle, earlier in the year in southern than in northern waters so that fishermen themselves would follow the northward drift. It is significant, in view of de Valera's thesis (1961, 243 and 250) that the impulses underlying the court and allied cairns of Ireland entered from the west, that mackerel (*Scomber scombrus*) tagged off Co. Cork are known to have passed up the west coast to south-west Scotland. At the very least sea fisheries, some at least established by Mesolithic man, need to be taken into account when seeking to understand the progress of geographical discovery and the consequent movement of ideas and people.

5

CONCLUSION

I began this book by asserting that the nineteenth-century division of the Stone Age into two stages, the Palaeolithic and the Neolithic, created a barrier to a just understanding of the course of prehistory (Clark 1978). I then went on to review some of the results that have followed from recognising that 'gap' and 'revolution' were equally illusory and that the Stone Age was in reality continuous. This was done in relation first to the origins of economies based primarily on cereal farming and stock-raising in south-west Asia and next to the process of Neolithisation by which agriculture and the manufacture of pottery were adapted by the inhabitants of Mediterranean and Temperate Europe.

I would now like to conclude with a few reflections of a more general nature. The notion of gaps and jumps are equally untenable. History is of its essence continuous and its pre-historic periods form no exception. The notion that prehistoric man suddenly acquired a new dimension, the possibility of becoming civilised, at the very moment he started to grow wheat and barley, or for that matter rice, maize, manioc, squash or beans, as controlled crops, would be false even if such a moment had ever in fact occurred. The real turning points in human affairs were primarily biological and social (Clark 1978). The first, which made all else possible, was the emerg-ence, during a later stage of the Upper Pleistocene, but still of the order of forty thousand years ago, of *Homo sapiens sapiens*, the species to which all existing races of man belong (Clark

1979). The second, the emergence of stratified from segmental societies, which made possible the growth of advanced civilisations and states, many of them recording their own histories, was itself made possible by the changes in the basis of subsistence wrought over long ages by Mesolithic man and his counterparts in different parts of the world.

It was the appearance of beings in every respect the physical and, so far as we can tell from the surviving data, the psychological equals of modern man that marked the key turning point. An enhanced degree of self-awareness combined with an ability to symbolise in no way inferior to our own, if we may judge from the cave art or the indications of notation from Upper Palaeolithic Europe, made possible the later course not merely of prehistory but of history itself. It is well to remember that even on a material level Neanderthal man himself had expanded as far north as the tundra zone of Russia, and that, with the conspicuous exception of the islands of the Pacific Ocean, almost the whole of the rest of the world had been explored and occupied by his successor *Homo sapiens sapiens* before ever a crop had been sown. Man did not become fully sapient when he assumed the burden of tilling the soil. It was the other way round. His sentence to hard labour followed from his desire to know the difference between right and wrong.

The ingenuity with which the advanced hunters and foragers of the Late Pleistocene and their successors adapted to a multiplicity of environments was such that their techniques and strategies were capable of securing not merely an adequate but frequently a gratifying way of life solely on the basis of hunting, fishing and foraging. So much indeed was this the case that such economies were still being practised in many parts of the world down to their colonisation by Europeans. The peoples who depended on the so-called predatory economies were every bit as well endowed in a biological sense as those who developed economies based primarily on farming. This is sufficiently obvious if one reflects that the long process culminating in the domestication of animals, plants and not least of men themselves can hardly have been carried out in any other way than through the intensification and ultimately the transformation of earlier systems, or by any other people than those of the Archaic, Mesolithic or in whatever other way designated Intermediate phase.

One implication of this is that the process of transformation already documented for parts of south-west Asia, Meso-america and coastal Peru, is likely to have gone forward else-where in the world. Every civilisation marked by the attain-ment of states must necessarily have rested on an economic base resulting from such transformation. This defines some of the major gaps in our knowledge of world prehistory. Certainly we shall never understand the earliest peasant societies of India, China or south-east Asia until the immedi-ately antecedent phases of their prehistories have been much more fully understood. Intensive research needs to be con-centrated on the Mesolithic or Intermediate phase in the pre-history of all those parts of the world that supported advanced cultures. The study of this phase will alone provide clues to the genesis of the several diverse civilisations of mankind as well as helping to account for the varying ways in which these were diffused to, and received and modified by, the indigenous populations of the huge territories marginal, as Europe was itself to begin with, to their emergence. Whether Matyushin was justified in rating the Mesolithic phase of prehistory so highly is certainly open to dispute. What is undoubtedly true is that the Intermediate phase of the Stone Age stands in urgent need of research in most parts of the World.

BIBLIOGRAPHY

Acanfora, M. A. (1962-3) Gli scavi di Valle Ottara presso Citta-
    ducale. *Bull. Paletnologia* NS XIV, vol.71-2.
Albrethsen, S. E. & E. B. Petersen (1976) Excavation of a mesolithic
    cemetery at Vedbaek, Denmark. *Acta Archaeol.* 47, 1-28.
Alexander, J. (1972) *Yugoslovakia before the Roman Conquest.*
    London.
Anati, E. (1963) *Palestine before the Hebrews.* London.
Aparisi, J. San Valero (1950) *La Cueva de la Sarsa.* Valencia.
Arribas, A. (1966) Le néolithique ancien de la Péninsule Ibérique.
    Palaeohistoria XII, 11-16.
Bagniewski, Z. (1973) Das Mesolithikum in Niederschlesien, in
    The Mesolithic in Europe (ed. S. K. Kozłowski) pp.23-52.
    Warsaw: University Press.
Bagolini, B. & P. Biagi (1977) Current culture history issues in the
    study of the neolithic of northern Italy. *London Inst.
    Archaeol. Bull.* no.14, 143-66.
Bailloud, G. & P. M. de Boofzheim (1955) *Les Civilisations Néo-
    lithiques de la France.* Paris.
Bandi, H-G. *et al.* (1964) *Birsmatten-Basigrötte. Eine mittelsteinzeit-
    liche fundstelle im unteren Birstal.* Acta Bernensa I. Berne.
Bárta, J. (1957) Pleistocénne piesočné duny pri Seredi a ich paleo-
    litické a mezolitické osídlenie. *Slovenská Archeológia* V, I.
Becker, C. J. (1954) Stenalderbebyggelsen ved Store Valby i
    Vestsjaelland. *Aerbøger*, 127-97.
Berciu, D. (1961) *Contribuţil la problemele Neoliticului în Romínia în
    lumina noilór cercetări.* Bucharest.
Bohmers, A. & A. Bruijn (1958/9) Statistische und graphische
    Methoden zur Untersuchung von Flintcomplexen. IV.
    Das lithische Material aus dem bandkeramischen Sied-
    lungen in den Niederlanden. *Palaeohistoria* VI/VII,
    183-212.

Bibliography

Bowen, E. G. (1972) *Britain and the Western Seaways*. London.

Braidwood, R. J. (1973) Prehistoric investigations in south-western Asia. *Proc. Amer. Phil. Soc. 116*, 310-20.

—— (1975) *Prehistoric Man*, 8th edn. Chicago.

Braidwood, R. J. & B. Howe (1960) *Prehistoric Investigations in Iraqi Kurdistan*. Chicago: University Press.

Bray, W. (1976) From predation to production: the nature of agricultural evolution in Mexico and Peru, in *Problems in Economic and Social Archaeology* (eds Sieveking, Longworth & Watson) pp.73-95. London: Duckworth.

Brea, L. B. (1946/56) *Gli Scavi nella Caverna delle Arene Candide*, 2 vols. Bordighera.

—— (1949) La cueva Corruggi en el territorio de Pachino. *Ampurias* XI, 1-23.

—— (1950) Il neolitico a ceramica impressa e la sua diffusione nel Mediterraneo. *Riv. Studi Liguri* XVI, 25-36.

Breuil, H. & G. Zbyszewski (1947) Revision des industries mésolithiques de Muge et de Magos (Collections du Service Géologique du Portugal). *Com. Serviços Geologicos de Portugal* XXVIII, 149-96. Lisbon.

Brøndsted, J. (1938) *Danmarks Oldtid. I. Stenalderen*. Copenhagen.

Brothwell, D. (1975) Salvaging the term 'domestication' for certain types of man/animal relationship: the possible value of a eight-point system. *J. Archaeol. Sci. 2*, 397-400.

Brown, A. (1893) On the continuity of the neolithic and palaeolithic periods. *J. Roy. Anthropol. Inst.* XXII, 66-98.

Brown, D. F. (1965) The chronology of the northwestern Mediterranean, in *Chronologies in Old World Archaeology* (ed. R. W. Elrich) pp.321-42. Chicago: University Press.

Burkitt, M. (1925) The transition between palaeolithic and neolithic times. *Proc. Prehist. Soc. E. Anglia* V, 16-33.

—— (1926) *Our Early Ancestors*. Cambridge.

Bushnell, G. H. S. (1977) The beginning and growth of agriculture in Mexico, in *The Early History of Agriculture* (eds Sir Joseph Hutchinson & Grahame Clark) pp.117-20. London: British Academy.

Buzy, D. (1928) *Rev. Biblique*, 557-78.

Byers, D. S., ed. (1967) *The Prehistory of the Tehuacan Valley*, vol.1, *Environment and Subsistence*. Texas: University Press.

Chaplin, R. E. (1969) The use of non-morphological criteria in the study of animal domestication from bones found on archaeological sites, in *The Domestication of Plants and Animals* (eds P. J. Ucko & G. W. Dimbleby) pp.231-45. London.

Childe, V. G. (1931) The forest cultures of northern Europe: a study in evolution and diffusion. *J. Roy. Anthropol. I.* LXI, 325-48.

—— (1935a) Changing methods and aims in prehistory. *Proc. Prehist. Soc.* I, 1-15.

—— (1935b) *The Prehistory of Scotland.*

—— (1947) *The Dawn of European Civilization*, 4th edn (1st edn 1929). London.

Chmielewski, W. (1952) *Zagadnienie, Grobowćow Kujawskich w Świetle Ostatnich Badán.* Lodz.

Clark, J. G. D. (1932) *The Mesolithic Age in Britain.* Cambridge.

—— (1936) *The Mesolithic Settlement of Northern Europe.* Cambridge.

—— (1939) *Archaeology and Society.*

—— (1946) Seal-hunting in the Stone Age of north-western Europe: a study in economic prehistory. *Proc. Prehist. Soc.* XII, 12-48.

—— (1947) Whales as an economic factor in prehistoric Europe. *Antiquity* XXI, 84-104.

—— (1948a) Fowling in prehistoric Europe. *Antiquity* XXII, 116-30.

—— (1948b) The development of fishing in prehistoric Europe. *Ant. J.* XXVIII, 45-85.

—— (1952a) *Prehistoric Europe. The Economic Basis* (revised 1974). London: Methuen.

—— (1952b) Die mittlere Steinzeit, in *Historia Mundi* (Fritz Kern) Bd.I, 318-45.

—— (1953) The economic approach to prehistory. *Proc. Brit. Acad.* XXXIX, 215-38.

—— (1958) Blade and trapeze industries of the European Stone Age. *Proc. Prehist. Soc.* XXIV, 24-42.

—— (1963) Neolithic bows from Somerset, England, and the prehistory of archery in north-western Europe. *Proc. Prehist. Soc.* XXIX, 50-98.

—— (1965) Radiocarbon dating and the expansion of farming culture from the Near East over Europe. *Proc. Prehist. Soc.* XXXI, 58-73.

—— (1967) *The Stone Age Hunters.* London: Thames & Hudson.

—— (1970) *Aspects of Prehistory.* London: U. California Press.

—— (1972a) *Star Carr : a case study in bioarchaeology.* Addison-Wesley Module in Anthropology no.10.

—— (1972b) The archaeology of Stone Age settlement. *Ulster J. Archaeol.* 35, 3-16.

—— (1975) *The Earlier Stone Age Settlement of Scandinavia.* Cambridge.

—— (1976) Prehistory since Childe. *Bulletin* no.13, 1-21. London: University Institute of Archaeology.

—— (1977a) The economic context of dolmens and passage-graves in Sweden, in *Ancient Europe and the Mediterranean* (ed. V. Markotic) pp.35-49. Warminster: Aris & Phillips.

—— (1977b) *World Prehistory in New Perspective* (illus. 3rd edn). Cambridge.

—— (1978) Neothermal orientations, in *The Early Postglacial Settlement of Northern Europe* (ed. P. Mellars) pp.1-10. London: Duckworth.

—— (1979) Primitive man as hunter, fisher and farmer, in *The Origins of Civilization* (ed. P. R. S. Moorey) pp.1-21. Oxford: Clarendon Press.

Clark, J. G. D. & M. W. Thompson (1953) The groove and splinter technique of working antler in Upper Palaeolithic and Mesolithic Europe. *Proc. Prehist. Soc.* XIX, 148-60.

Clark, J. G. D., *et al.* (1950) Preliminary report on excavations at Star Carr . . . (second season, 1950). *Proc. Prehist. Soc.* XVI, 109-29.

—— (1954) *Excavations at Star Carr Mesolithic Site at Seamer, near Scarborough, Yorkshire.* Cambridge.

Clarke, D (1976) Mesolithic Europe: the economic basis, in *Problems in Economic and Social Anthropology* (ed. G. de G. Sieveking *et al.*) pp.449-81. London: Duckworth.

Clason, A. T. (1967) The animal bones found at the LBK settlement at Bylany. *Arch. Rozhledy 19*.

Clutton-Brock, J. (1962) Near Eastern canids and the affinities of the Natufian dog. *Tierzücht ZüchtBiol. 76*, 326-33.

Coles, J. M. (1971) The early settlement of Scotland: excavations at Morton, Fife. *Proc. Prehist. Soc.* XXXVII, 284-366.

Coon, C. S. (1951) *Cave Explorations in Iran 1949.* Philadelphia: Univ. of Pennsylvania Mus.

Coulanges, L. (1935) Les gisements préhistoriques de Sauveterre-la-Lémance (Lot-et-Garonne). *Arch. de l'Inst. de Pal. Hum.*, Mém.14.

Dakaris, S-I., E. S. Higgs & R. W. Hay (1967) The climate, environment and industries of stone age Greece, part 1. *Proc. Prehist. Soc.* XXX, 1-28.

Daniel, M. & R. Daniel (1948) Le Tardenosien classique du Tardenois. *L'Anthropologie* LII, 411-49.

de Fonton, M. E. (1966) Origine et développement des civilisations néolithiques Mediterranéennes en Europe occidentale. *Palaeohistoria* XII, 209-48. Groningen.

Degerbøl, M. (1961) On a find of a preboreal domestic dog (*Canis familiaris* L.) from Star Carr, Yorkshire, with remarks on other mesolithic dogs. *Proc. Prehist. Soc.* XXVII, 35-65.

de Mortillet, A. & G. (1881) *Musée Préhistorique*. Paris.

de Mortillet, G. (1883) *Le Préhistorique Antiquité de l'Homme*. Paris.

de Valera (1961) The 'Carlingford Culture', the long barrow and the neolithic of Great Britain and Ireland. *Proc. Prehist. Soc.* XXVII, 234-52.

Ducos, P. (1958) Le gisement de Châteauneuf-les-Martigues. Les mammifères et les problèmes de domestication. *Bull. musée d'Anthrop. Préhist. de Monaco 5*, 119-33.

Egloff, M. (1965) *Jhb. d. Schweiz. Ges. f. Ur. und Fruhgeschichte 52*, 59-66.

Evans, J. D. (1958) 13th *Ann. Rep. Inst. Archaeology London*.

—— (1959) The prehistoric culture-sequence in the Maltese archipelago. *Proc. Prehist. Soc.* XIX, 41-94.

—— (1964) Excavations in the neolithic settlement of Knossos, 1957-60. Part I. *Ann. Brit. School Archaeol. Athens 59*, 132-240.

—— (1968) Knossos neolithic, Part II. *Ann. Brit. School Archaeol. Athens 63*, 239-76.

Evans, J. D. & C. Renfrew (1968) *Excavations at Saliagos near Antiparos*. London.

Fodera, V. (1961) *The Sicilian Tuna Trap*. Studies and Reviews, General Fisheries Council for the Mediterranean no.15. Rome: F.A.O.U.N.

Formazov, A. A. (1955) Periodization of mesolithic sites in the USSR in Europe. *Sovetskaya Arkheologiya* XXI, 38-51.

Garašanin, M. V. (1958) Neolithikum und Bronzezeit in Servien und Makedonien. *Ber. d. Rom.-Germ. Komm. 39*, 189.

Garrod, D. A. E. (1930) The palaeolithic of southern Kurdistan: excavations in the caves of Zarzi and Hazr Merd. *Am. School Prehist. Res. Bull.* no.6, 8-43.

—— (1957) The Natufian Culture: the life and economy of a Mesolithic people in the Near East. Reckitt Archaeological Lecture, *Proc. Brit. Acad.*, 211-27.

Garrod, D. A. E. & D. M. A. Bate (1937) *The Stone Age of Mount Carmel. Excavations at the Wady el-Mughara*, vol.1. Oxford.

—— (1942) Excavations at the cave of Shukbah, Palestine, 1928. *Proc. Prehist. Soc.* VIII, 1-20.

Gersbach, E. (1956) Ein Harpunenbruchstück aus einer Grube der jüngeren Linearbandkeramik. *Germania 34*, 266-70.

Gimbutas, M. (1956) *The Prehistory of Eastern Europe*. Harvard.

Bibliography

Glob, P. V. (1952) *Danske Oldsager. Yngre Stenalder.* Copenhagen.

Godwin, H. (1956) *The History of the British Flora.* Cambridge.

Guilaine, J. (1979) The earliest neolithic in the west Mediterranean: a new appraisal. *Antiquity* LIII, 22-30.

Gurina, I. I., ed. (1966) Sources of ancient culture (mesolithic epoch). *Mat. Issled. po Arkh. SSSR* no. 126.

Hammond, N. (1977) The early history of American agriculture: recent research and current controversy, in *The Early History of Agriculture* (eds Sir Joseph Hutchinson & Grahame Clark) pp.120-8. London: British Academy.

Heere, W. (1969) The science and history of domestic animals, in *Science in Archaeology* (eds Brothwell & Higgs). London.

Helbaek, H. (1960) Ecological effects of irrigation in ancient Mesopotamia. *Iraq* 22, 186-96.

—— (1966) Pre-pottery neolithic farming at Beidha, in Kirkbride (1966) appendixes A to D, 61-6.

Higgs, E. S. (1968) The stone industries of Greece, in *La Préhistoire, Problèmes et Tendences*, pp.223-35. Paris: Centre National de la Recherche Scientifique.

—— ed. (1972) *Papers in Economic History.* Cambridge.

—— (1974) *Palaeoeconomy.* Cambridge.

Higham, C. W. (1968) Patterns of prehistoric economic exploitation on the Alpine foreland. *Vierteljahrsschrift de Naturf. Ges. in Zürich*, Jhg.113, Hft.1, 41-92.

Hole, F. & K. V. Flannery (1967) The prehistory of southwestern Iran: a preliminary report. *Proc. Prehist. Soc.* XXXIII, 147-206.

Hole, F., K. V. Flannery & J. Neely (1969) *Prehistory and Human Ecology of the Deh Luran Plain, an Early Village Sequence from Khuzistan, Iran.* Memoirs Mus. of Anthropology, Univ. of Michigan, no.1. Ann Arbor.

Holmberg, E. J. (1964) *The Neolithic Pottery of Mainland Greece.* Göteborgs Kungl. Vetenskaps-och Vitterhets-Samhälles Handl. 6th Series, Ser.A, Bd.7, no.2.

Hopf, M. (1969) Plant remains and early farming in Jericho, in *The Domestication and Exploitation of Animals and Plants* (eds P. J. Ucko & G. W. Dimbleby) pp.355-9.

Höppener, H. (1931) *Halieutica. Bijdrage tot de Kennis der Oud-Grieksche visscherij.* Amsterdam.

Jacobsen, T. W. (1969) Excavations at Porto Cheli and vicinity, preliminary report. II: the Franchthi Cave, 1967-68. *Hesperia* XXXVIII, 343-81.

—— (1972) Excavations in the Franchthi Cave, 1967-71. *Hesperia* XLII, 45-88 and 253-83.

Jarman, M. R. (1972) European deer economies and the advent of
the neolithic, in *Papers in Economic Prehistory* (ed. E. S.
Higgs) pp.125-47. Cambridge.

—— (1977) Early animal husbandry, in *The Early History of
Agriculture* (eds Sir Joseph Hutchinson & Grahame Clark)
pp.85-93. London: British Academy.

Jarman, H. N., A. J. Legge & J. A. Charles (1972) Retrieval of plant
remains from archaeological sites by froth flotation, in
Papers in Economic Prehistory (ed. E. S. Higgs) pp.49-64.
Cambridge.

Jazdzewski, K. (1938) Gräberfelder der bandkeramischen Kultur
und die mit ihnen verbundenen Siedlungspuren in Brześc
Kujawski. *Wiadomósci Archaeologiczhe 15*, 1-105.

Kaelas, L. (1953) *Den äldre megalitkeramiken under mellan-neo-
litikum i Sverige*. Stockholm.

—— (1966) The megalithic tombs in south Scandinavia – migra-
tion or cultural influence? *Palaeohistoria* XII, 287-321.

Keller, F. (1866) *The Lake Dwellings of Switzerland and other parts
of Europe.*

Kenyon, K. M. (1957) *Digging up Jericho*. London.

—— (1959) Early Jericho. *Antiquity* XXXIII, 1-9.

Kidder, A. V. & T. Esaka (1968) *Jōmon Pottery*. Tokyo.

Kirkbride, D. V. W. (1958) A Kebaran rock shelter in Wadi Made-
magh, near Petra, Jordan. *Man*, 55-8.

—— (1966) Five seasons at the pre-pottery neolithic village of
Beidha in Jordan. A summary. *Palestine Exploration Q.*,
8-72.

Klima, B. (1957) Übersicht über die jüngsten paläolithischen
Forschungen in Mähren. *Quartär* IX, 85-130.

Kozłowski, S. K. (1972) *Prehistory of the Polish Territories between
the 9th and the 5th Millenium B.C.* Warsaw.

Kozłowski, S. K. & E. Sachse-Kozłowska (1975) The system of
providing flint raw materials in the late palaeolithic in
Poland, in *Second Int. Symposium on Flint* (ed. F. H. G.
Engelen). Maastricht.

Krainov, D. A. (1960) The cave site Tash-Air as a basis for dividing
the late palaeolithic Crimean culture into periods. *Matt. i
Issled. p. Arkh. SSSR* no.91.

Lacam, R., A. Niederlender & H. V. Vallois (1944) Le gisement
mésolithique du Cuzoul de Gramat. *Arch. de l'Inst. de
Hum.*, Mém.21. Paris.

Lanfranchi, F. de & M-C. Weiss (1973) *La Civilisation de Corse.
Les Origines*. Ajaccio.

Bibliography

Lartet, E. & H. Christy (1875) *Reliquiae Aquitanicae; being contributions to the Archaeology and Palaeontology of Perigord and the adjoining provinces of Southern France.* London.

Legge, A. J. (1972) Prehistoric exploitation of the gazelle in Palestine, in *Papers in Economic Prehistory* (ed. E. S. Higgs) pp.19-24. Cambridge.

Leisner, V. (1966) Die verschiedenen phasen des Neolithikums in Portugal. *Palaeohistoria* XII, 363-72.

Leisner, G. & V. Leisner (1943) *Die Megalithgräber des Iberischen Halbinsel: Der Suden.* Berlin.

—— (1951) *Autas do Concelho de Reguengos de Monsaraz.* Lisbon.

Lepiksaar, J. (1971) Benbestämninger. *Fynd*, 523-5.

Leroi-Gourhan, A., J. & N. Chavaillou (1963) Paléolithique du Péloponnèse. *Bull. Soc. Préhist. Francaise*, 249-65.

Libby, W. F., E. C. Anderson & J. R. Arnold (1949) Age determination by radiocarbon content: world-wide assay of natural radiocarbon. *Science 109*, no.2827, 227-8.

Löhr, H. (1975) Zur Verbreitung von Fuerstein aus der Bergwerken in der Umgebung von Maastricht in Deutschland, in *Second Int. Symposium on Flint* (ed. F. H. G. Engelen). Maastricht.

Lollini, D. G. (1965) Il neolitico nelle Marche alle luce delle recente scoperte, in *Atti VI Congr. Int. delle Scienze Preistorische* (1962) II, 309-15. Rome.

MacBurney, C. B. M. (1976) *Early Man in the Soviet Union.* Reckitt Archaeological Lecture. London: British Academy.

McGhee, R. & J. A. Tuck (1975) An archaic sequence from the strait of Belle Isle, Labrador. *Archaeological Survey of Canada*, paper no.34, 85-92. Ottawa.

MacNeish, R. S., A. Nelken-Terner & I. W. Johnson, eds (1967) *The Prehistory of the Tehuacan Valley* vol.2, *Nonceramic Artifacts.* Texas: University Press.

Mathiassen, T. (1939) Bundsø, en Yngre Stenalders Boplads paa Aals. *Aarbøger*, 1-195.

—— (1940) Havnelev-Strandegaard. Et Bidrag til Diskussionen om den yngre Stenalders Begyndelse i Danmark. *Aarbøger*, 1-55.

Mathyushin, G. I. (1976) *Mezolit Yuzhnogo Urala.* Moscow: Nauka.

Mellaart, J. (1967) *Catal Hüyük. A Neolithic Town in Anatolia.* London.

Milojčić, V. (1949) *Chronologie der jungeren Steinzeit Mittel- und Sudosteuropas.* Berlin.

Milojčić, V., J. Boessneck & M. Hopf (1962) *Die Deutschen Aus-grabungen auf der Argissa-Magula in Thessalien. Das Präkeramische Neolithikum sowie die Tier und Pflanzenreste.* Bonn.

Milojčić, V., J. Boessneck, D. Jung & H. Schneider (1965) *Paläo-lithikum um Larissa in Thessalien.* Bonn.

Mongait, A. (1959) *Archaeology in the USSR.* Moscow. (Pelican Edition, London, 1961.)

Mortensen, P. (1962) On the chronology of early village-farming communities in Northern Iraq. *J. Directorate Gen. of Antiquities, Iraq,* XVIII, 73-80.

—— (1970) A preliminary study of the chipped stone industry from Beidha, an early neolithic village in southern Jordan. *Acta Arch.* XLI, 1-54.

Nandris, J. (1970) The development and relationships of the earlier Greek neolithic. *Man* NS 5, no.2, 192-213.

—— (1978) Some features of neolithic climax societies. *Studia Praehistorica 1-2,* 198-211. Sofia.

Neuville, R. (1951) Le paléolithique et le mésolithique du désert de Judée. *Arch. de l'Inst. Pal. Hum.,* no.24. Paris.

Newell, R. R. (1970) The flint industry of the Dutch linearband-keramik, in *Linearbandkeramik aus Elsloo und Stein* (P. J. R. Modderman) ch.VI. Amersfoort.

Nøe-Nygaard, N. (1974) Mesolithic hunting in Denmark illustrated by bone injuries caused by human weapons. *J. Archaeol. Sci. I,* 217-48.

Nordmann, V. (1936) *Menneskets Indvandring til Norden* (English summary). Dan. Geol. Unders. r. III, nr.27. Copenhagen.

Noy, T., A. J. Legge & E. S. Higgs (1973) Excavations at Naḥal Ören, Israel. *Proc. Prehist. Soc.* XXIX, 75-99.

Obermaier, H. (1924) *Fossil Man in Spain.* New Haven. (Translated from *El Hombre Fosil,* Madrid, 1916. The 1924 edition was brought up to date to mid-1922.)

Oeschger, H. *et al.* (1970) *Radiocarbon 12,* 379f.

Ophoven, M., E. della Santa & J. Hamal-Nandrin (1948) *Utilisation à l'âge de la pierre mésolithique du grès-quartzite dit de Wommersom.*

Păunescu, A. (1970) *Evoluţia uneltor şi armelor de piatră cioplită descoperite pe teritoriul României.* Bucharest.

Payne, S. (1972) Partial recovery and sample bias: the results of some sieving experiments, in *Papers in Economic Prehistory* (ed. E. S. Higgs) pp.49-64. Cambridge.

Péquart, M. & St J. Péquart (1934) La nécropole mésolithique de l'Ile d'Hoëdic (Morbihan). *L'Anthropologie* XLIV, 1-20.

Bibliography

Péquart, M., St J. Péquart, M. Boule & H. Vallois (1937) Téviec. Station-nécropole mésolithique du Morbihan. *Arch. de l'Inst. Pal. Hum.*, Mém.18. Paris.

Pericot, L. (1942) *La Cueva del Parpalló.* Madrid.

—— (1945) La cueva de la Cocina (Dos Aguas) *Arch. Prehist. Levantina* 11, 39-71.

Perkins, D. (1964) Prehistoric fauna from Shanidar, Iraq. *Science* *144*, 1565-6.

Perrot, J. (1952) Têtes de flèches du natufian et du tahunien (Palestine). *Bull. Soc. Préhist. Française 49*, 439-49.

—— (1957) Le mésolithique de Palestine et les récentes découvertes à Eynam (Ain Mallaha). *Antiquity and Survival* 11, 91-110.

—— (1960) Excavations at 'Einan ('Ein Mallaha). Preliminary Report on the 1959 Season. *Israel Exploration Journal 10.*

—— (1966) Le gisement natoufien de Mallaha (Eynam), Israel. *L'Anthropologie 70*, 437-83.

—— (1968) La préhistoire Palestinienne. *Supplement au Dictionnaire de la Bible*, 286-446. Paris.

Peters, E. (1934) Das Mesolithikum der oberen Donau. *Germania 18*, 81-9.

Petersson, M. (1951) Mikrolithen als Pfeilspitzen. Ein Fund aus dem Lilla Loshult Moor, ksp. Loshult, Skåne. *Medd. Lunds Univ. Hist. Mus.*, 123-37.

Pidoplichko, I. G. (1969) *Late Palaeolithic Dwellings of Mammoth Bones in the Ukraine.* Kiev.

Piette, E. (1889) L'Epoque de transition intermédiaire entre l'âge du renne et l'époque de la pierre polie, in *Congr. Int. d'Anthr. et d'Arch. Préhist.*, *C.R. Xth sess.* Paris.

Piggott, S. (1937) The long barrow in Brittany. *Antiquity*, 441-55.

—— (1968) The earliest wheeled vehicles and the Caucasian evidence. *Proc. Prehist. Soc.* XXXIV, 266-318.

Renfrew, C., J. E. Dixon & J. R. Cann (1966) Obsidian and early cultural contact in the Near East. *Proc. Prehist. Soc.* XXXII, 30-72.

Ribiero, C. (1880) Les kioekkenmoeddings de la Vallée du Tage, in *Congr. Int. d'Anthr. et d'Arch. Préhist.*, Lisbon, pp.279-90.

Roche, Abbé J. (1960) *Le Gisement Mésolithique de Moita do Sebastião.* Lisbon.

Rodden, R. J. (1962) Excavations at the early neolithic site at Nea Nikomedeia, Greek Macedonia. *Proc. Prehist. Soc.* XXVIII.

Rozoy, J. G. (1973) The Franco-Belgian epipalaeolithic current problems, in *The Mesolithic in Europe* (ed. S. K. Kozłowski) pp.503-30. Warsaw: University Press.

Bibliography

Rozoy, J. G. (1978) Les derniers chasseurs. *Bull. Soc. Archaeol. Champenoise*, special no.

Rust, A. (1943) *Die Alt- und Mittelsteinzeitlichen Funde von Stellmoor*. Neumünster.

Salomonsson, B. (1960) Fouilles à Belloy-sur-Somme en 1952 et 1953. *Medd. Lunds. Univ. Hist. Mus.*, 5-109.

Savory, H. N. (1968) *Spain and Portugal*. London: Thames & Hudson.

Schetelig, H., & H. Falk (1937) *Scandinavian Archaeology* (trans. E. V. Gordon). Oxford: University Press.

Schietzel, K. (1965) *Müddersheim. Eine Ansiedlung der jüngeren Bandkeramik im Rheinland*. Köln.

Schmidt, R. R. (1912) *Die diluviale Vorzeit Deutschlands*. Stuttgart.

Schwantes, G. (1923) Das Beil als Scheide zwischen Palaolithikum u. Neolithikum. *Arch. Anthrop.* NF XX, Hft.1.

—— (1928) Nordisches Palaolithikum und Mesolithikum. *Arkiv. f. Volkerkunde in Hamburg* XIII, 159-252.

—— (1939) *Die Vorgeschichte Schleswig-Holsteins (Stein und Bronzezeit)*. Neumünster.

Smith, M. (1952) The mesolithic in the south of France: a critical analysis. *Proc. Prehist. Soc.* XVIII, 103-20.

Solecki, R. S. (1963) Prehistory in Shanidar Valley, northern Iraq. *Science 139*, 179-93.

Solecki, R. L. (1964) Zawi Chemi Shanidar, a post-pleistocene village site in northern Iraq. *Rep. VIth Congr. on Quaternary*, vol.IV, pp.405-12. Lodz.

Srejović, D. (1969) The roots of the Lepinski Vir culture. *Archaeologia Jugoslavica* X, 13-21.

—— (1972) *Europe's First Monumental Sculpture: New Discoveries at Lepinski Vir*. London: Thames and Hudson.

—— (1977) The Odmut Cave – a new facet of the mesolithic culture of the Balkan peninsula. *Archaeologia Jugoslavica* XV, 3-7.

Srejović, D. & Z. Letica (1978) *Vlasac. A Mesolithic Settlement in the Iron Gates*, vol.1 *Archaeology*. Belgrade.

Strömberg, M. (1971) *Die Megalithgräber von Hagestad*. Lund.

Sturdy, D. A. (1975) Some reindeer economies in prehistoric Europe, in *Paleoeconomy* (ed. E. S. Higgs). Cambridge.

Sulimirski, T. (1970) *Prehistoric Russia. An Outline*. London.

Taute, W. (1972) *Archäologische Information* I, 29-40.

Telegin, D. Ya. (1966) Mesolit levoberezhnoy Ukrainy . . ., in *U Istorov Drevnikh kultur (Epokha Mezolita)* (ed. I. I. Gurina) pp.99-107. Mat. i Issled. po Arkheologii SSSR, no.26.

Theocharis, D. R. (1973) *Neolithic Greece*. Athens.

Bibliography

Tichy, R. (1962) Osídlení s volutovou keramikou na Moravě. *Památky Archaeologické* LIII, 245-301.

Tringham, R. (1968) A preliminary study of the early neolithic and latest mesolithic blade industries in southeast and central Europe, in *Studies in Ancient Europe* (eds J. M. Coles & D. D. A. Simpson) pp.45-70. Leicester: University Press.

Troels-Smith, J. (1953) Ertebøllekultur-Bondekultur. Resultaten af de sidste 10 aars undersøgelser i Aamosen, Vestjaelland. *Aarbøger*, 5-62.

Turnbull, P. F. (1974) The fauna from the terminal pleistocene of Palegawra Cave, a Zarzian occupation site in north-eastern Iraq. *Fieldiana Anthropology 63*, no.3, 81-146.

Turville-Petre, F. (1932) Excavations in the Mughavet el-Kebarah. *J. Roy. Anthrop. Inst.* LXII.

Vaufrey, R. (1939) L'art Rupestre Nord-Africain 4-45. *Arch. de l'Inst. Pal. Hum.*, Mém.20. Paris.

Vita-Finzi, C. & E. S. Higgs (1970) Prehistoric economy in the Mount Carmel area of Palestine: site catchment analysis. *Proc. Prehist. Soc.* XXXVI, 1-37.

Voevodskii, M. V. (1950) *Kratkie soob. Inst. Ist. Mat. Kult.* XXXI, 96-119.

Völzing, O. (1935-8) *Fundberichte aus Schwabe*, NF 9.

Von Gonzenbach, V. (1949) *Die Cortaillodkultur in der Schweiz.* Basel.

Weinberg, S. S. (1965) The Stone Age in the Aegean. *Camb. Anc. Hist. I*, fasc.36. Cambridge.

Went, A. E. J. (1952) The Irish hake fishery, 1504-1842. *J. Cork Hist. Antiq. Soc.* V, no.III, 250-60.

Westropp, H. M. (1872) *Pre-historic Phases.* London.

Whitehouse, R. D. (1968) Settlement and economy in southern Italy in the neothermal period. *Proc. Prehist. Soc.* XXXIV, 332-67.

—— (1969) The neolithic pottery sequence in southern Italy. *Proc. Prehist. Soc.* XXXV, 267-310.

Wigforss, J. (1971) Stenäldersboplatsen Bua Västergård, Gröteborg. *Fynd*, 483-508.

Wyss, R. (1968) Das Mesolithikum, in *Ur. und Frühgeschichtliche Archäologie der Schweiz*, bd.1, pp.123-44. Zurich.

Zeuner, F. E. (1945) *The Pleistocene Period.* London: Ray Society.

Zohary, D. (1969) in *The Domestication and Exploitation of Plants and Animals* (eds P. J. Ucko & G. W. Dimbleby).

INDEX